Youth Edition

T·H·E
BONDAGE
BREAKER

Neil T. Anderson & Dave Park

HARVEST HOUSE PUBLISHERS
Eugene, Oregon 97402

THE BONDAGE BREAKER, YOUTH EDITION

Copyright © 1993 by Harvest House Publishers
Eugene, Oregon 97402

Library of Congress Cataloging-in-Publication Data

Anderson, Neil T., 1942–
    The bondage breaker / Neil T. Anderson, David Park.
    —Youth ed.
     p. cm.
    Includes bibliographical references.
    ISBN 1-56507-139-5
    1. Demonology—Juvenile literature. 2. Spiritual life—
Christianity—Juvenile literature. 3. Pastoral psychology—
Juvenile literature. 4. Mental illness—Biblical teaching—
Juvenile literature. [1. Devil. 2. Christian life. 3. Conduct
of life.]   I. Park, David, 1961– . II. Title.
BT975.A53   1993
235'.4—dc20   93-18871
                                          CIP
                                          AC

Printed in the United States of America.

To my parents,
Chub and Ruth Park,
and to Grace's parents,
Leon and Sharon DuPeire.
May God's truth shine the way for you.

—Dave

Acknowledgments

It has been three years since The Bondage Breaker *first came out in the adult edition. I had no idea that hundreds of thousands of people would be blessed by the message of this book. Hundreds of letters with wonderful testimonies of finding freedom in Christ have come to our office. At last count, the adult edition has been translated into 15 foreign languages. I will never forget the 4200 Filipinos and missionaries who attended a Bondage Breaker conference in Manila sponsored by Campus Crusade for Christ. What an incredible privilege and joy to see people find their freedom in Christ.*

I am eternally grateful and remain totally dependent upon the Lord Jesus Christ, the Bondage Breaker, who made all this possible. He is our life and the only hope we have for freedom.

I prayed for and waited a long time for the right person to be a part of the Freedom in Christ Youth Ministries. We needed someone who was mature and gifted enough to help young people find their freedom in Christ. The Lord brought us two, Rich Miller and Dave Park. Rich wrote The Slimeball Memos. *It will open your eyes to the spiritual battle going on in a fast-moving fictional way. Dave did the major work of revising this edition of* The Bondage Breaker. *What a joy to work with him. May the Lord use this book to set thousands of our young people free in Christ.*

—Neil

Since accepting Christ in 1976, God has brought a number of wonderful people into my life. God has used their mentoring, insights, and love to help shape me more like His wonderful Son.

I want to thank Mark Noble for leading me to Christ. Also, Terry Rudd, Rick Kouba, Lynn Jones, Bill Noble, Mark Bailey, and Dr. Bud Hopkins for training me by making God's Word come alive in their lives.

I am deeply grateful to Josh McDowell for the opportunity to serve with him side by side and observe his ministry. Your wisdom and insights have forever touched my life.

To Neil and Joanne, your love and lives constantly minister to me. Thank you!

I appreciate the whole staff of Harvest House Publishers, especially Eileen Mason and Barb Sherrill. And to Ed Stewart, thanks for another job well done.

I am indebted to the whole Freedom in Christ team, particularly Pam Maxwell and Roger McNichols.

And to Grace, David, Ashley, and Dani—I love you!

—Dave

Contents

Foreword by Josh McDowell
Free at Last!

Part One: Take Courage!

Part Two: Stand Firm!

Part Three: Walk Free!

Foreword
by Josh McDowell

As a young person today you have two absorbing concerns. First, you desperately want to gain some sense of identity. Second, you want to experience the freedom to really walk with God. Few people are pointing you in the right direction, back to the pages of the Bible. Only in God's Word can you gain a sense of who you really are, and how significant and secure you are as a child of God.

I have shared many times in my speaking and writing about my own personal struggles with a poor self-image. I can say without any hesitation that the realization of who I am in Christ is the single most important element in my successful walk as a Christian and in ministry.

Neil and Dave have developed two much-needed books that point you to the one place where you can gain your true identity and freedom. Your commitment to the Word of God and careful study will help you realize the power of your identity in Christ and help you become the spiritual person you want to be.

How wonderful it is to see resources specifically written for youth—*The Bondage Breaker, Youth Edition* and *Stomping Out the Darkness*—that address the real issues with which many young people are struggling. Standing against the spiritual forces of this fallen world and learning how to win the battle for the mind is a message that should not have any age limit.

Jesus promised us that we could live a victorious, abundant, and free life. I believe those promises were made to young people as well. Neil and Dave show in a warm and insightful way how our God is in the business of *Stomping Out the Darkness* and how Jesus Christ is the *Bondage Breaker*.

These books are must reading for every young person who desires to walk free and understand the truth of who he or she really is in Christ.

Free at Last!

A few years ago I (Neil) was speaking in a church about the New Age movement. I spoke from 1 Timothy 4:1: "But the Spirit explicitly says that in later times some will fall away from the faith, paying attention to deceitful spirits and doctrines of demons." After my message, people crowded around me wanting to hear more about freedom from spiritual problems caused by demonic attack.

Sitting about halfway back in the church was a 22-year-old woman who had been crying uncontrollably since the service ended. Several people had tried to comfort her, but she wouldn't allow anyone to get near her. Finally a church staff member cut through the crowd around me and said, "I'm sorry, folks, but we need Dr. Anderson back here right away."

As I approached the young woman I could hear her sobbing, "He understands! He understands!" We were able to get her out of the sanctuary and into a private office. After she calmed down, I set up a time when we could meet together.

When Nancy arrived for her appointment her face was marked by ugly, open scratch wounds. "I've been scratching myself like this, and I can't control it," she admitted with embarrassment.

Nancy described her horrible childhood, which included an abusive father and a grandmother who identified herself as a black witch. "When I was three years old I received my guardians—spirit guides," she continued. "They were my companions, telling me how to live and what to say. I never questioned if having spirit guides was anything but normal until my mother took me to Sunday school. Then I began to suspect that my inner companions might not be good for me. When I asked my parents about it, my father beat me. I never asked again!"

In order to deal with the increasing torment that her spirit guides brought to her life, Nancy resorted to rigid personal discipline. In her high school years she trusted Christ as her Savior. But instead of leaving her, her "guardians" continued to harass her.

After high school Nancy joined the Marines to become even more disciplined. Determined to be the toughest lady Marine, she won awards for her discipline. But her spiritual torment kept pushing her mind and emotions to the edge. She refused to tell anyone about her mental battle for fear that she would be labeled insane.

Finally the pressure overcame her and she snapped. Nancy quietly accepted a medical discharge and retreated to a lonely life of inner turmoil and pain. This was Nancy's condition when she came to church and heard me talk about deceiving spirits.

"Finally someone understands me!" Nancy said tearfully.

"Would you like to get rid of your spirit guides?" I asked.

There was a long pause. "Will they really leave, or will I go home and be thrashed by them again?"

"You will be free," I assured her.

An hour later Nancy *was* free—and was hugging us with an openness she had never known before. "Now I can have people over to my house!" she exclaimed joyfully.

Nancy's experience is not uncommon. We have ministered to more Christians in bondage to the dark side of the spiritual world than you may believe. We have discovered that many Christians are totally unprepared to deal with the dark world of Satan's kingdom or to minister to those who are in bondage to it.

God Wants You
Mature and Free

There are two concepts that determine the victory and fruitfulness of a Christian. The first concept is *maturity*. Paul wrote: "We are to grow up in all aspects into Him, who is the head, even Christ . . . to a mature man, to the measure of the stature which belongs to the fulness of Christ" (Ephesians 4:15,13). God has given us everything we need to grow to maturity in Christ (2 Peter 1:3).

But Satan is trying to stop us from growing. He and his demons will do anything he can to keep us from realizing who we are and what we have in Christ. They are unseen spiritual forces, not physical enemies we can fight with human strength (Ephesians 6:12). But we must experience victory over the dark side before we can fully mature.

Our book, *Stomping Out the Darkness* (Regal Books), focuses on a young believer's walk by faith and maturity in Christ. It also exposes the strategies Satan uses to block our growth. The book deals with the basic issues of our identity in Christ and gives practical steps on how to live by faith, walk according to the Spirit, renew our mind, manage our emotions, and resolve the emotional problems of our past through faith and forgiveness. We strongly suggest that you read through *Stomping Out the Darkness* along with your study of this book.

The second concept of the successful Christian life is *freedom*, which is the central theme of *The Bondage Breaker—Youth Edition*. Paul declared: "It was for freedom that Christ set us free; therefore keep standing firm and do not be subject again to a yoke of slavery" (Galatians 5:1). This verse not only assures us that God wants us free, but also warns us that we can lose our freedom if we fail to stand firm in our faith.

Before we received Christ, we were slaves to sin. But because of Christ's work on the cross, sin's power over us has been broken. Satan no longer owns us, and he has no right to tell us what to do. He is a defeated foe, but he is committed to keeping us from realizing that. He knows he can block our victory as Christians if he can deceive us into believing that we are nothing but sinful failures controlled by our habits.

As long as Satan can confuse us and blind us with his dark lies, we won't be able to see that the chains that once had us bound are broken. We are free in Christ, but if the devil can deceive us into believing we're not, we won't experience the freedom which is our inheritance.

There's no such thing as instant maturity, but freedom from Satan's crippling lies is completely possible and can usually be accomplished in a short time. Once a person is free, it is amazing how quickly he or she matures!

In this book we want to describe the spiritual battle we're in and explain how young Christians can find victory in Christ. Part One explains our position of freedom, protection, and authority in Christ. Part Two warns that very real and very personal demonic powers are trying to rob us of our freedom by tempting us, accusing us, and deceiving us. Part Three presents the steps to freedom in Christ which will help you walk free of the enemy's schemes to block your growth and freedom.

Are you one of those Christians who lives in discouragement and defeat because you are ruled by fear, anger, depression, habits you can't break, thoughts or inner voices you can't get away from, or sinful behavior you can't seem to overcome? We're not saying that every spiritual problem is the result of direct demonic activity. But we are saying that many Christians are not experiencing their freedom in Christ because they have not accepted the reality of the spiritual world nor understood the battle that is going on for their mind.

Your inheritance in Christ is the complete freedom He promises in the Bible, as shown in the testimony of Nancy and many others you will read about in the pages ahead. We want to introduce you to the One who has already overcome the darkness and secured your freedom: Jesus Christ the Bondage Breaker!

PART ONE

Take Courage!

1

You Don't Have to Live in the Shadows

I (Neil) remember counseling a young Christian who was in deep spiritual, mental, and emotional confusion. At one point before I began meeting with her, she wrote the following prayer, then ten minutes later tried unsuccessfully to kill herself with an overdose of pills:

Dear God,

Where are You? How can You watch and not help me? I hurt so bad, and You don't even care. If You cared You'd make it stop or let me die. I love You, but You seem so far away. I can't hear You or feel You or see You, but I'm supposed to believe You're here. Lord, I feel them and hear them. They are here. I know You're real, God, but they are more real to me right now. Please make someone believe me, Lord. Why won't You make it stop? Please,

Lord, please! If You love me You'll let me
die.

A Lost Sheep

We have met hundreds of young Christians like
the one who wrote this sad note. Most of them
didn't attempt suicide as this one did, but many of
them talked about dark desires to do so. And nearly
all of them admitted to the presence of "them"—
inner urges or voices which bothered them, tempted
and taunted them, accused them, or threatened them.

The fact that people struggle with negative or
opposing thoughts is well accepted. We often caution young people who make appointments to talk
with us that they may have opposing thoughts such
as, "Don't go; they can't help you." Or distracting
thoughts will pop into their minds like, "I don't
want to go" or "I've tried this before and it didn't
work." One person wrote to Neil: "Every time I try
to talk to you, or even think about talking to you, I
completely shut down. Voices inside literally yell at
me: 'No!' I've even considered killing myself to end
this terrible battle going on inside. I need help!"

We asked 1292 Christian high school students in
a survey, "Have you heard 'voices' in your head like
there was a subconscious self talking to you, or have
you struggled with really bad thoughts?" Seventy
percent answered yes! If you struggle with tempting
or accusing thoughts in your head, you're not alone.
You may not have told anyone about your experiences because you fear that people would think
you're a mental case. Maybe you have kept quiet
because *you* think you're crazy. Maybe you have

been taught that Christians can't have these kinds of problems.

But the time has come for us to wake up to the fact that Satan is real and that demons exist. If you hear tormenting voices in your head or feel a dark presence in your room at night (and 47 percent of those surveyed have), you're not crazy; you're under attack. You need to know how to defend yourself against Satan's fiery darts. That's what this book is all about.

Many Christians don't complain about hearing voices, but their minds are filled with such confusion that their daily walk with Christ is completely discouraging. When they try to pray they begin thinking about a million things they should be doing. When they sit down to read the Bible or a good Christian book they can't concentrate.

When they have an opportunity to serve the Lord in some way they give up because of discouraging thoughts of self-doubt: "I'm not a strong Christian"; "I don't know enough about the Bible"; "I'm too young"; "I have too many sinful thoughts." Instead of being victorious, dynamic Christians full of joy, they trudge through life under a cloud just trying to hang on until Jesus comes. Some of this discouragement is certainly our own faulty thinking, but it can also reflect deception from the enemy.

Common False Beliefs About Bondage

Where do the evil voices, bad thoughts, guilty feelings, and confusion come from? One of the main reasons so many youth are in bondage today is because they don't know the answers to these questions. They are living under a number of false beliefs about the spiritual world which must be corrected. Here is what some Christians falsely believe—and Satan loves it.

1. *Demons were busy when Christ was on earth, but they're not around much today.* Young Christians who believe this after reading what God's Word says and seeing what is going on in the world today are not facing the facts. The New Testament clearly says that believers will wrestle "against the rulers, against the powers, against the world forces of this darkness, against the spiritual forces of wickedness in the heavenly places" (Ephesians 6:12). Paul goes on to describe every piece of spiritual armor we are to put on in order to defend ourselves against "the flaming missiles of the evil one" (verses 13-17). If dark spiritual powers are no longer attacking believers, why would Paul warn us about them and insist that we arm ourselves against them?

The powers and forces that Paul wrote about are still around today. You can see it around your school. How many kids do you know who are involved in New Age practices, Ouija boards, astrology, occult games like Dungeons and Dragons, or music with evil lyrics?

The kingdom of darkness is still present, and Satan wants to make our lives miserable and keep us from walking strong and tall in Christ. If you don't believe that Satan and his demons are present and busy, then either God or you will have to take a bum rap for all the evil Satan is dumping on you and the rest of the world.

2. *What early Christians called demonic activity is only mental illness.* If one of your friends reported hearing inner voices or sensing a dark presence in his room, most secular counselors would say, "He has a mental problem; he's paranoid." Very few would think it's a spiritual problem, the activity of Satan's demons. Why? Because a natural explanation is the best such counselors can do without a belief in God or the existence of Satan.

The world's understanding of our problems is incomplete. It ignores the reality of the spiritual world.

Not all physical, mental, and emotional problems young Christians experience are specifically demonic. But ignoring the presence and influence of Satan and his demons will leave many problems unsolved.

3. *Some problems are psychological and some are spiritual.* This false belief suggests that the human soul and spirit are separate, which isn't true. There is no problem that isn't psychological, because there is never a time when our mind, emotions, and will are not involved. And there is no problem that isn't spiritual, because there is no time when God is not present or when it is safe for us to take off the armor of God.

Saying that a problem is only psychological overlooks how God and Satan are involved. Saying that a problem is only spiritual ignores our responsibility for how we must think, feel, and choose. In order to deal with our inner conflicts we must consider both the psychological and spiritual influences which are at work.

4. *Christians can't be attacked by demonic forces.* This is a lie that the devil would love us to swallow so we will drop our defenses against him. If Satan can't touch Christians, why are we told to put on the armor of God, to resist the devil, to stand firm, and to be alert? If we can't be deceived by Satan, why does Paul talk about our relationship to the powers of darkness as a wrestling match? Those who say the enemy can't influence us are deceived.

5. *The activity of demons is only seen in weird behavior or gross sin.* There are still cases of demon activity today like the wild, demon-possessed man called "Legion" in Luke 8:26-39. But most young Christians under spiritual attack lead fairly normal lives while experiencing serious inner problems for which no cause or solution has been found. Since they think that satanic attack only affects mass murderers or violent sex criminals, these ordinary people wonder what's wrong with them and why they can't just "do better."

Satan's first and best strategy is deception. Paul warned: "Satan disguises himself as an angel of light. Therefore it is not surprising if his servants also disguise themselves as servants of righteousness" (2 Corinthians 11:14,15). It is not the few weird or violent people who are the main problem. Rather, it is Satan's subtle deception and invasion into the lives of "normal" believers like us that keeps us from being effective.

6. *Freedom from spiritual bondage is the result of a power encounter with demonic forces.* Freedom from spiritual problems and bondage is not a power encounter;

it's a truth encounter. Satan is a liar, and he will work undercover at all costs. But the truth of God's Word exposes him and his lies. His demons are like cockroaches that scurry for the shadows when the light comes on. Satan's power is in the lie, and when his lie is exposed by the truth, his plans are foiled. Satan's power was broken at the cross. He is a defeated foe.

Then how can he be so effective? Let me illustrate with a story from childhood.

When I (Neil) was a boy on the farm, my dad, my brother, and I would visit our neighbor's farm. The neighbor had a yappy little dog that scared the socks off me. When it came barking around the corner, my dad and brother stood their ground, but I ran. Guess who the dog chased! I escaped to the top of our pickup truck while the little dog yapped at me from the ground.

Everyone except me could see that the little dog had no power over me except what I gave it by not standing up to it. The dog had no power to throw me up on the pickup; it was my belief that put me up there. That dog controlled me by using my mind, my emotions, my will, and my muscles, all of which were motivated by fear. Finally I gathered up my courage, jumped off the pickup, and kicked a small rock at the mutt. And it ran!

Satan is like that yappy little dog: He deceives us into fearing him more than God. His power is in the lie. He is the father of lies (John 8:44) who deceives the whole world (Revelation 12:9). As a result, the whole world is under the influence of the evil one (1 John 5:19).

The devil can do nothing about who you are in Christ. But if he can deceive you into believing his lies about you and God, you will spend a lot of time on top of the pickup truck! You don't have to outshout him or outmuscle him to be free of his control. You just have to *outtruth* him. Believe, declare, and act upon the truth of God's Word, and you will ruin Satan's strategy.

This concept has had a dramatic effect on our counseling. Often when a spiritual conflict was exposed in someone being counseled, it would turn into a power encounter. Persons would become unconscious, run out of the room, or start behaving like they were crazy. The common first approach was to get the demon to expose itself, then command it to leave. This process was often very difficult for the person. And though progress was made, the process would usually have to be repeated.

We have learned from the Bible and from our experience that truth, not power, is what sets people free. The power of Satan is in the lie, and the power of the believer is in knowing the truth. We are to pursue truth, not power.

Also, persons in bondage are not liberated by what the counselor does but by what they do. It's not what Neil or Dave or your pastor or youth leader believes that breaks Satan's grip on your life, it's what *you* believe. And what you believe must be the truth. Notice the following verses:

You will know the truth, and the truth will set you free (John 8:32 NIV).

[Jesus said] I am the way, and the truth, and the life (John 14:6).

But when He, the Spirit of truth, comes, He will guide you into all the truth (John 16:13).

[Jesus prayed to the Father] I'm not asking you to take them [Christians] out of the world, but to keep them safe from Satan's power.... Make them pure and holy through teaching them your words of truth (John 17:15,17 TLB).

Stand firm then, with the belt of truth buckled around your waist (Ephesians 6:14 NIV).

Finally, brethren, whatever is true . . . let your mind dwell on these things (Philippians 4:8).

When God first disciplined the early church in Acts 5, He did so in a dramatic way. Two people dropped dead when their sin was discovered. What was the issue: drugs, sex? No, the issue was *truth*. Peter confronted Ananias and Sapphira: "Why has Satan filled your heart to lie to the Holy Spirit?" (verse 3). God wanted the church to know that Satan the deceiver can ruin us if he can get us to believe and live a lie. That's why it is so important to take "every thought captive to the obedience of Christ" (2 Corinthians 10:5).

Setting Captives Free

Before Jesus died on the cross and rose from the

dead, God empowered Him and His hand-picked disciples to take authority over demonic powers in the world. But something radical happened at the cross and in the resurrection that permanently changed the way we encounter spiritual forces.

First, Jesus' death and resurrection defeated and disarmed the rulers and authorities of the kingdom of darkness (Colossians 2:15). Before the cross, "all authority . . . in heaven and on earth" had not yet been given to Christ. But Matthew 28:18 assures us that the resurrected Christ now has all authority. Because of the cross Satan is defeated, and he has no authority over those who are in Christ. Believing the truth of Christ's victory and Satan's defeat is the first step to successfully putting down the enemy's attempts to discourage and hassle you.

Second, in Christ's death and resurrection every believer is made alive with Him and is now seated with Him (Ephesians 2:5,6). You no longer need someone else—like a pastor or youth leader—to take authority over Satan for you. You now reside in Jesus Christ, who has all authority. In order to resist the devil, you need to understand and exercise your position and authority in Christ.

Freedom is your inheritance as a Christian. That's why Paul wrote:

> I pray that your hearts will be flooded with light so that you can see something of the future he has called you to share. I want you to realize that God has been made rich because we who are Christ's have been given to him! I pray that you will begin to understand how incredibly great his power is to

help those who believe him. It is the same mighty power that raised Christ from the dead and seated him in the place of honor at God's right hand in heaven, far, far above any other king or ruler or dictator or leader. Yes, his honor is far more glorious than that of anyone else either in this world or the world to come (Ephesians 1:18-21 TLB).

When Satan harasses you, you may want to crawl under a rock in misery, like the girl whose prayer note opened this chapter. You may cry out for God to deliver you, like Jesus miraculously and instantly delivered the demonized people in the Gospels. But your deliverance has already been accomplished because of Christ's work on the cross and His resurrection. That's the good news Paul was trying to tell us about in his prayer. Since you are with Christ in the light, you never again need to live in the shadows.

But it is your responsibility to choose the truth and resist the devil. From your position in Christ, you must resist the devil, renounce (which means to turn your back on) any ways by which you have participated in his schemes, confess your sin, and forgive those who have offended you. These critical steps to freedom are the focus of Part Three of this book.

The woman who called herself "A Lost Sheep" at the beginning of this chapter finally gained God's view of her condition. Four years after she wrote her desperate prayer, she wrote this response based on her new understanding of God's provision in Christ. Her words are based on Scripture. Allow them to shine some light into the shadows of your life.

My Dear Lost Sheep,

You ask Me where I am. My child, I am with you and I always will be. You are weak, but in Me you are strong. I love you so much that I can't let you die. I am so close that I feel everything you feel.

I know what you are going through, for I am going through it with you. But I have set you free and you must stand firm. You do not need to die physically for My enemies to be gone, but be crucified with Me and I will live in you, and you shall live with Me. I will direct you in paths of righteousness. My child, I love you and I will never forsake you, for you are truly mine.

Love, God

Truth Encounter

Read: John 8:32; John 14:6; John 16:13

Reflect: 1. Could you relate to the Christians in this chapter who felt spiritually oppressed? What experiences have you had?

2. Have you been exposed to any of the misconceptions talked about in this chapter? Did you accept any of them as true? How did those misconceptions affect your life?

3. Do you feel you fully understand how to use your authority in Christ and resist the devil? What are some ways you can learn more about your authority in Christ?

4. Do you ever feel that your personal walk with Christ is incomplete or that you're not growing? In what ways?

Respond: Take a few moments to pray and ask the Lord to reveal to your mind any misconceptions that you might have about bondages or the spiritual world around us. Ask the Lord to replace any deceptions you might have with His truth. Ask Him to help you grow in your understanding of who you are in Christ.

2
Finding Your Way in the World

In high school I (Dave) read William Golding's chilling novel, *Lord of the Flies*. Perhaps you have read it in an English or literature class. The book is about a group of boys stranded on an island without adult supervision. They start out treating each other with kindness and respect as they were taught. But eventually the evil side of their natures takes control, resulting in hatred, violence, and even murder.

The book's title is actually taken from a biblical reference to Satan. Beelzebub, one of Satan's names in the Bible, literally means "lord of the flies." This is one of the most descriptive titles for the devil in Scripture. Satan is like a pesky, disease-carrying fly, out to harass and infect every believer with his temptations, accusations, and lies.

This picture of Satan was strongly impressed on my wife, Grace, and me one summer when we returned home after a three-week trip. Our first clue that something was very wrong came when we opened the front door and a swarm of flies came buzzing out. The flies were followed by a strong smell that smacked us square in the face. It was obvious that something inside was very dead.

By the time we reached the kitchen we were gagging from the smell. And there on the floor in front of our freezer was the source. Somehow the freezer door had come open and a frozen chicken had fallen out. The rotten bird was nearly twice its original size, and it pulsed and bubbled as if it were alive. During the three weeks we were gone the chicken had thawed and been transformed into a maternity hospital for flies. When I tried to scoop up the smelly carcass with a dustpan, it burst open and thousands of squirmy maggots spilled out onto the floor. We almost passed out!

This gross picture illustrates what Satan is like. He swarms around people who are spiritually dead or living out of harmony with God. He plants his lies in our minds, and if we don't resist him with the truth, his evil ideas eat away at us like maggots, tearing us down.

Golding would have us believe that the "lord of the flies" is the evil, beastly side of human nature, not Satan, the being who rules the dark side of the spiritual world. Satan would like us to believe that he doesn't really exist and that evil is just a human weakness. In fact, Satan doesn't want us to believe that the spiritual world exists at all.

But Golding's picture of evil is incomplete. We have three very present and personal enemies: the evil influences of the world, the flesh (our tendency to run our own lives without God), and—most overlooked today—the devil. Satan is a real but unseen being. He and his demons are alive and active in our world today. But, as illustrated by William Golding's novel, he has been very successful in convincing people that they are evil and that he, the evil one, doesn't exist.

While Christians have been questioning the reality of Satan and the influence of demons, many have charged full speed into the dark side of the spiritual world. The New Age movement teaches that we are gods and can create reality with our minds. New Age channelers (who are really spiritual mediums) can be heard on radio and TV talk shows bragging about their spirit guides (which are really demons).

Parapsychology (study of the occult) is becoming accepted as a "science" in our universities. Fascination with the supernatural continues to grow, as seen in the popularity of movies like *Ghostbusters*, *Field of Dreams*, *Ghost*, *Poltergeist*, and *The Exorcist*. The seductive power of Satanism is increasingly evident in our culture.

Fascination with the supernatural is even growing in our Christian schools. Twenty-six percent of the Christian high schoolers we surveyed have played with a Ouija board, 20 percent have tried astrology, 16 percent have played Dungeons & Dragons, and 12 percent have had their palms read.

The curiosity of the occult and the lure of supernatural knowledge and power has trapped many in Satan's web. To avoid this trap we must understand this world from God's perspective.

The Two-Level Worldview

What is your worldview? Maybe you've never heard

that term before. A worldview is how you understand the world around you and how you relate to it. In other words, a worldview is like a pair of glasses through which you see what is happening in the world. Your worldview is what you believe about reality.

The Western world (North America and parts of Western Europe) sees reality in two levels (see Figure 2a). The upper level is the hidden, unseen world which is understood through religion and spiritual experiences. The lower level is the natural world which is understood through science and the physical senses.

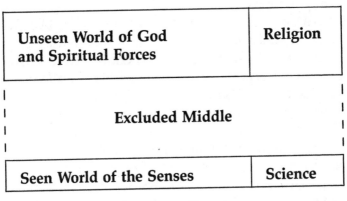

Unseen World of God and Spiritual Forces	Religion
Excluded Middle	
Seen World of the Senses	Science

Figure 2a

For those of us educated in the West, we have been taught that the spiritual, unseen world has no practical effect on the natural world. It has been left out from our understanding of reality. We have been taught to trust only that which we can see, hear, touch, taste, smell, and measure in a laboratory. Many ignore, doubt, or laugh at the idea of evil spirits having an impact on us. Some may say they believe in God but see Him as uninvolved with human affairs.

In contrast to the West, two-thirds of the people of the world hold an Eastern worldview. They believe that spiritual forces are an everyday reality. These people please their gods with peace offerings and perform religious rituals to ward off evil spirits. To the common people in Third World nations, religious practice or superstition is more practical in daily life than science.

It is easy for those of us raised in the West to say the Eastern worldview is wrong because of all the "success" of the Western world. *But both are worldly systems and neither reflects what the Bible says is real.*

Between the two levels is what Dr. Paul Hiebert, a missions expert, calls the "excluded middle." This is the real world where spiritual forces are active in the physical world. We must include the spiritual world, including the kingdom of darkness, in our worldview because in reality there is no excluded middle!

To show how this two-level thinking has affected the beliefs of some Western Christians, let me (Neil) tell you about a bright young woman named Dee, a pastor's daughter. Dee developed physical symptoms which were later diagnosed as multiple sclerosis. When I heard about Dee's condition and the prospect of her life with this crippling disease, I looked for an opportunity to talk to her.

"When did you first become aware of the symptoms?" I asked.

"Right after a special time of devotions I had with the Lord," Dee replied.

"What was so special about your devotions that day?"

"I was feeling sorry for myself when I read the passage where Paul told about his thorn in the flesh. Paul said God's power was perfected in his weakness, and I wanted God's power in my life too. So I asked for a thorn in the flesh."

"You asked God for a thorn in the flesh?" I tried to hide my shock.

"Yes."

"Do you know what Paul's thorn in the flesh was?"

"Some sort of physical problem, wasn't it?"

"Well, we're not told how it showed itself, but 2 Corinthians 12:7 clearly states that it was an angel of Satan—a demon! Paul never asked for it. In fact, he prayed three times that it be removed. Dee, I think Satan took advantage of your unscriptural prayer and afflicted you with these symptoms. I strongly recommend that you renounce your request for a thorn in the flesh and pray that any influence by Satan be removed from your life."

Dee received my counsel and we prayed together. She began to feel better almost immediately. The symptoms disappeared and she resumed her normal activities. Several months later the symptoms began to reappear. At that time I led her through a more thorough procedure of the steps to freedom as described in Part Three of this book. Today Dee is free.

Her father's first reaction to Dee's illness was typical of many Western Christians who look only for a natural explanation: "I never even considered Dee's condition to be a spiritual problem." For the same reason, some people argue that Dee's "recovery" was remission of a physical disease instead of freedom from a demonic activity.

Many Christians either exclude the supernatural from their worldview or believe that it has no effect on their lives. By doing so they exclude God's power from their beliefs and practices. They also explain all human problems—even those brought about by demonic influence, such as Dee's symptoms—as the result of mental or physical causes.

Living in the Excluded Middle

The Christian worldview looks at life through the Bible, not through culture or experience. The Bible clearly teaches that supernatural, spiritual forces are at work in the natural world. For example, approximately one-fourth of all the healings talked about in the Gospel of Mark were actually deliverances from demonic activity. The woman whom Jesus healed in Luke 13:11,12 had been the victim of a "sickness caused by a spirit" for 18 years.

In addition to Dee and her symptoms, many people we have counseled came with physical problems which disappeared shortly after the demonic influence was dealt with. The most common physical symptoms we have seen are headaches, dizziness, inability to read and concentrate on the Word of God, and general pain throughout the body.

We're not saying that everyone who is ill or in pain is being terrorized by a demon. That's going overboard toward the unseen spiritual level. But some Christians battle physical symptoms unsuccessfully through natural means when the basic problems and solutions are spiritual. By all means, go see your doctor who will test and treat you physically, *and* see your pastor who should be able to test and treat you spiritually.

Jesus left us "in the world" (John 17:11) to wrestle against "spiritual forces of wickedness in the heavenly places" (Ephesians 6:12). We live in the natural world, but we are involved in a spiritual war. The excluded middle is only excluded in our worldly minds, not in reality.

Getting Spiritual Without God

Young people in the West have begun to sense that there is more to life than what natural science has revealed. On the surface this new hunger may sound encouraging to those of us with a Christian worldview. But many who are unsatisfied by the materialistic world are often unhappy with organized religion. Instead of turning to Christ and His church, they are trying to fill their spiritual emptiness with the occult, parapsychology, Eastern religions, and numerous cults marching under the banner of the New Age movement.

Trying to meet spiritual needs apart from God is nothing new. The center of this unbiblical worldview is self: What will *I* get out of this? Who will meet *my* needs? I'm doing *my own* thing. Even a Christian who acts this way is motivated by selfish ambition and pride.

The apostle Peter is a clear example of the struggle between self and Christ-centered living. Only moments after Peter confessed the important truth that Jesus Christ is the Messiah, the Son of the living God

(Matthew 16:13-16), he found himself taking sides with the powers of darkness. When Jesus announced that suffering and death awaited Him at Jerusalem, "Peter took Him aside and began to rebuke Him, saying, 'God forbid it, Lord! This shall never happen to You'" (verse 22).

Jesus responded: "Get behind Me, Satan! You are a stumbling block to Me; for you are not setting your mind on God's interests, but man's" (verse 23).

Jesus' put-down seems cold and severe. But His remark clearly describes the nature of the advice Peter tried to give: "Save yourself at all costs. Watch out for yourself. Don't do anything that is painful or inconvenient."

Peter's advice was from Satan, for Satan's primary aim is to get us all to center our lives on our own interests. But the Christian worldview has a different center. Jesus confronts our self-serving motives and offers the view from the cross. Only from this perspective can you escape the bondage of Satan, whose sole intent is "to steal, kill, and destroy" (John 10:10).

The View from the Cross

Adam was the first human to entertain the idea that he could "be like God" (Genesis 3:5), which is the core of the self-centered worldview that Satan promotes. Countless others since Adam have been tempted by Satan into believing that they are their own gods, and today the New Age movement is promoting this lie in a big way.

However, the biblical account of creation clearly shows us that only God the Creator is truly God. Adam and his ancestors are not gods; we are created beings which cannot live apart from God. The idea that man is his own god is the heartbeat of the Satan-inspired worldview and the primary link in the chain of spiritual bondage to the kingdom of darkness.

The problem with man's attempt at being his own god is that he was never designed to be a god. He lacks the needed qualities to take care of his own life and future. Even sinless, spiritually alive Adam in the garden of Eden wasn't equipped to be his own god, much less those of us born since then, who come into the world spiritually dead. Contrary to what the New Agers tell us, the ability to be a god never was in us, isn't in us now, and never will be in us. Being God is something that belongs to God alone.

If you desire to live in freedom from the bondage of the world, the flesh, and the devil, this important link in the chain must be smashed. The self-centered worldview which Satan and his demons are promoting all around you must be replaced by the teachings of Jesus. We must understand what Jesus taught to His disciples after Peter's self-preserving rebuke:

> If anyone wants to be a follower of mine, let him deny himself and take up his cross and follow me. For anyone who keeps his life for himself shall lose it; and anyone who loses his life for me shall find it again. What profit is there if you gain the whole world—and lose eternal life? For I, the Son of Mankind, shall come with my angels in the glory of my Father and judge each person according to his deeds (Matthew 16:24-27 TLB).

The following six guidelines from Jesus' statement make up the view from the cross. They are the needed guidelines for those who would be free from the bondage of the world system and the devil who inspires it. Stay within the light of the victory of the cross and you will successfully find your way in a dark world.

Deny Yourself

Denying yourself is not the same as self-denial. Every athlete practices self-denial, restricting himself from certain foods, drugs, alcohol, all-night parties, and anything else which keeps him from reaching his goals. But the ultimate purpose of self-denial is self-promotion: to win a game, to break a record, to achieve athletic status and recognition.

Jesus was talking about denying yourself in the struggle over who is going to be God in our lives. Jesus doesn't enter into that battle; He's already won it. He occupies the throne and graciously offers to share it with us. But we want to be king in our lives. Until we deny ourselves that which was never meant to be ours—the role of being God in our lives—we will never be at peace with ourselves or God, and we will never be free.

You were not designed to function without God, nor was your soul designed to work as a master. You will either serve God and His kingdom or Satan and his kingdom. When you deny yourself, you invite God to take the throne of your life, to occupy what is rightfully His, so that you may live as a person who is spiritually alive in Christ. Denying yourself is essential to spiritual freedom.

Pick Up Your Cross Daily

The cross we are to pick up on a daily basis is not our *own* cross but *Christ's* cross. We are closely identified with His cross, however, because we have been crucified with Christ and no longer live; Christ lives in us (Galatians 2:20). His cross provided forgiveness from what we have done and deliverance from what we were. We are forgiven because He died in our place; we are delivered because we died with Him. We are both justified (made acceptable to God) and sanctified (set apart for a holy purpose) as a result of the cross.

To pick up the cross daily means to realize every day that we belong to God. We have been purchased by the blood of the Lord Jesus Christ (1 Peter 1:18,19). When we pick up the cross we are saying that our identity and purpose is not based in our physical life but in our relationship with God.

Follow Christ

We follow Christ by being led by the Holy Spirit to the death of self-rule. As Paul wrote: "We who live are constantly being delivered over to death for Jesus' sake, that the life of Jesus also may be manifested in our mortal flesh" (2 Corinthians 4:11).

You might be thinking, "Dying to self-rule doesn't sound like fun to me. In fact, it sounds awful." Well, it's not. It is a tremendous victory when we stop trying to play God, and let God be the Lord of our lives, our problems, and our future. Being led by the Spirit of God is our assurance that we are His children (Romans 8:14). Only when we come to the end of our resources do we discover God's resources.

We were not designed to function independently of God. Only when we are dependent on Him and intent on following Christ are we complete and free to prove that the will of God is good, acceptable, and perfect (Romans 12:2). "Deny yourself, pick up your cross daily, and follow Me" may seem like you are sacrificing yourself and gaining nothing. Nothing could be further from the truth, for what are you really sacrificing?

Sacrifice the Lower Life to Gain the Higher Life

If you want to save your natural life (in other words, find your identity and sense of self-worth in positions, titles, accomplishments, and possessions, and seek only worldly well-being), you will lose it. At best you can only possess these earthly values for a lifetime, only to lose everything for eternity. Furthermore, in all your efforts to possess these earthly treasures, you will fail to gain all that can be yours in Christ.

I (Dave) received a letter from a teenager who made this important discovery:

> Dear Dave,
>
> In our conversation about my grades in sociology and chemistry, you said something that really made me think. You said, "Don't let it be pride." At first I felt offended. Why? Because I had believed so thoroughly that grades would bring me worth. I believed this so much that I had taken grades and let them become a god to me. I thought that good grades could be my defense against my

insecurities. I felt I was good enough because
of my grades.

After talking with you I realized I was
deceiving myself. I wasn't walking in the
Spirit. Now I know that it's God, not my
grades, who makes me secure, accepted, and
significant. If I am honestly humble, *He* will
lift me up and reward me.

Shoot for this world and that's all you'll get, and
eventually you will lose even that. But shoot for the
next world and God will throw in this one as a bonus.
Paul made a similar statement: "Bodily discipline is
only of little profit, but godliness is profitable for all
things, since it holds promise for the present life and
also for the life to come" (1 Timothy 4:8).

Sacrifice the Pleasure of Things to Gain the Pleasure of Life

What would you accept in trade for the fruit of the
Spirit in your life? What material possession, what
amount of money, what position or title would you exchange for the love, joy, peace, and patience (Galatians 5:22) that you can have if you abide in Christ?
"Nothing," we would all probably agree. The lie of
this world is that fame and possessions will bring us
the fruit of the Spirit. Where is the majority of our time
and energy being spent: on temporary things or eternal things? It seems to be the great ambition of man to
be happy as animals instead of being blessed as children of God.

Jesus talked about this very conflict with two of
His closest friends, Mary and Martha (Luke 10:38-42).

During Jesus' visit, Martha was caught up in material things, focusing on preparing and serving a meal, while Mary centered her attention on Jesus and His words. Martha's tendency was to love things and use people, but Jesus indicated that Mary had chosen "the good part" (verse 42) by loving people and using things. Victory over self comes as we learn to love people and use things, and not get those two activities mixed up.

Sacrifice the Temporary to Gain the Eternal

Possibly the greatest sign of spiritual maturity is the ability to postpone rewards. The flesh wants instant gratification, but the more you try to satisfy its lusts, the less hope you have for the future. The more you feed a lust, the larger it grows, and you will end up sacrificing the eternal to gain the temporal. Hebrews 11:24-26 says: "By faith Moses, when he had grown up, refused to be called the son of Pharaoh's daughter; choosing rather to endure ill-treatment with the people of God than to enjoy the passing pleasures of sin; considering the reproach of Christ greater riches than the treasures of Egypt; for he was looking to the reward." Even if following Christ results in tough times in this life, He will make it right in eternity.

Satan's ultimate lie is that you are capable of being the god of your own life, and bondage is living as though his lie is true. Satan is out to take God's place in your life. And whenever you live independently of God, focusing on yourself instead of Christ, seeking material and worldly things over spiritual and eternal things, he has succeeded. The world's answer to this conflict of identity is to puff up the ego while denying God His rightful place as Lord. Satan couldn't be more pleased—that was his plan from the beginning.

Truth Encounter

Read: Matthew 16:24-27

Reflect: 1. How is the secular worldview affecting your understanding of Satan's activity in the world?

2. Do you know people who are seriously involved in the New Age or in the occult? What effect is it having on their lives?

3. Why do you think we have so much trouble denying ourselves, picking up our cross daily, and following Jesus? What are some practical ways you can pick up your cross daily and follow Jesus?

4. What are some of the temporary pleasures Satan uses to distract us from following Christ?

Respond: Pray and ask the Lord for insight as to how you deny yourself, pick up your cross daily, and follow Him. Ask the Lord to bring to mind special ways you can sacrifice the temporary things in life to gain the eternal.

3

You Have Every Right to Be Free

Lydia was dealt a bad hand in life right from the beginning. Memories of sexual abuse as a young child have haunted her continually throughout her Christian life. When she came to see me (Neil), her damaged self-image seemed beyond repair. As she told me her story, Lydia displayed little emotion, but her words reflected total despair.

"Who are you, Lydia? How do you see yourself?" I asked.

"I'm evil," she answered. "I'm just no good for anybody. People tell me I'm evil, and all I do is bring trouble."

"You're not evil," I argued. "How can a child of God be evil? Is that how you see yourself?" Lydia nodded.

I reached for a printed sheet of paper containing a number of statements describing who we are in Christ based on verses in the Bible and handed it to Lydia. (These statements are included in Chapter 13 in the "Who Am I?" list.) "Would you read these statements aloud right now?" I asked. "They will remind you of what the Bible says about you, and who you are in Christ."

Lydia took the paper and began to read the first statement aloud rather haltingly: "I am th-the s-s-salt of the . . ." Suddenly her character changed. She looked up and sneered, "No way, you dirty son of a —!"

It is never nice to see the evil one show his ugly personality through a victim like Lydia. But I took authority over him through prayer in Christ's name and led Lydia through the steps to freedom described in Part Three of this book. She was able to gain a new understanding of who she really is in Christ. She began to see herself as the product of the work of Christ on the cross instead of the victim of her past.

Satan had deceived Lydia into believing she was worthless and evil, which was a lie. He was dead set against her reading those statements of truth about her identity as a child of God. He knew that God's truth would uncover his lie just as surely as the light dispels the darkness. And he wasn't about to give up without a fight.

Nothing is more basic to our freedom from Satan's bondage than understanding what God has done for us in Christ and who we are as a result. Our attitudes, actions, responses, and reactions to life's circumstances are determined by how we see ourselves. If you see yourself as the helpless victim of Satan and his schemes, you will probably live like his victim and be in bondage to his lies. But if you see yourself as the dearly loved and accepted child of God that you really are, you will live like a child of God.

In this chapter we want to outline who we are in Christ. These concepts are key to our freedom from spiritual conflict as children of God.

You Are Eternally Alive and Well

Each of us is made up of at least two major parts: our outer self and our inner self. On the outside we have a physical body, and on the inside we have a soul/spirit. The soul describes our ability to think (mind), to feel (emotions), and to choose (will). The spirit describes our ability to relate to God. Our body is united with our soul/spirit, and that makes us physically alive. As Christians, our soul/spirit is united with God, and that makes us spiritually alive.

When God created Adam, he was totally alive— physically and spiritually. But because of Adam's sin and spiritual death, every person who comes into the world is born physically alive but spiritually dead. Being separated from God, we lacked the wisdom of God in our lives, so we learned to live independently of God, centering our interests on ourselves. Our learned independence from God is referred to in the Bible as the flesh.

When we were born again, our soul/spirit was united with God and we came alive spiritually, as alive as Adam was in the garden before he sinned. We are now in Christ, and Christ is in us. Since Christ who is in us is eternal, the spiritual life we have received from Him is eternal. We don't have to wait until we die to get eternal life; we possess it right now! And contrary to what Satan would like us to believe, he can't ever take eternal life away from us because he can't take Jesus away from us, who promised never to leave us or forsake us (Hebrews 13:5).

You Are Changed from Sinner to Saint

Have you ever heard a Christian say, "I'm just a sinner saved by grace"? Have you referred to yourself that way? If you see yourself as a sinner you will probably sin. What would you expect a sinner to do? There will be little in your life to distinguish you from a non-Christian, and you will be filled with feelings of defeat.

Satan will seize that opportunity, pour on the guilt, and convince you that you are doomed to a roller-coaster spiritual life. As a defeated Christian you will confess your sin and try to do better, but inwardly you will admit that you are just a sinner saved by grace, hanging on until Christ returns for you.

Is that who you really are? No way! The Bible doesn't refer to believers as sinners, not even sinners saved by grace. Believers are called saints—holy ones—who sometimes sin. We become saints at the moment of salvation—that's called justification. We live and grow as saints in our daily experience—called sanctification—as we continue to affirm who we really are in Christ. Seeing yourself as a saint instead of a sinner will have a powerful, positive effect on your daily ability to have victory over sin and Satan.

You Have Been Given God's Divine Nature

Ephesians 2:1-3 describes our nature *before* we came to Christ: "You were dead in your trespasses and sins, in which you formerly walked according to the course of this world, according to the prince of the power of the air. . . . and were by nature children of wrath." Before we became Christians our very nature was sin, and the result of our sin was death (separation from God).

But at salvation God changed us. We received "the divine nature, having escaped the corruption that is in the world by lust" (2 Peter 1:4). You are no longer in the flesh; you are in Christ. You had a sinful nature because you were separated from God, but now you are a partaker of Christ's divine nature. You didn't *become* God, but you received God's divine nature.

Paul said it this way: "You were formerly darkness, but now you are light in the Lord; walk as children of light" (Ephesians 5:8); "Therefore if any man is in Christ, he is a new creature" (2 Corinthians 5:17). In the face of Satan's accusations that we are no different, we must believe and live in harmony with the fact that we are eternally different in Christ.

The New Testament refers to the person we were before we received Christ as our "old self." When we received Christ as Savior, our old self, which lived independently of God, died (Romans 6:6). Our new self, inspired by our new identity in Christ and committed to live in dependence on God, came to life (Galatians 2:20).

Our old self had to die in order to end our relationship with sin which controlled it. Being a new person doesn't mean that we are sinless (1 John 1:8). But since our old self has been crucified and buried with Christ, we no longer *need* to sin (1 John 2:1). We sin when we choose to act independently of God.

You Can Be Victorious Over the Flesh and Sin

When our old sinful self died, sin's rule as our master ended. But sin is still around. It is strong and appealing, but its power and authority have been broken (Romans 8:2).

Also, our flesh, that part of us which was trained to live independently of God before we met Christ, did not die either. We still have memories, habits, and thought patterns in our brain which tempt us to focus on our own interests. We are no longer *in the flesh* as our old self was; we are now *in Christ*. But we can still choose to *walk according to the flesh* (Romans 8:12,13), obeying those old urges to serve ourselves instead of God.

It is our task to crucify the flesh (Romans 8:13) on a daily basis by learning to walk according to the Spirit (Galatians 5:16) and by replacing our old thought patterns with new patterns based on God's Word. That process is called "renewing our mind" (Romans 12:2).

Romans 6:11 summarizes what we are to believe about our relationship to sin because of our position in Christ: "Even so consider yourselves to be dead to sin, but alive to God in Christ Jesus." It doesn't matter whether we feel dead to sin or not; we are to *consider* it so because it *is* so. When we choose to believe what is true about ourselves and sin, and walk on the basis of what we believe, our right relationship with God will work out in our experience.

After teaching us what to *believe* about sin, Paul teaches us how to *relate* to sin: "Therefore do not let sin reign in your mortal body that you should obey its lusts, and do not go on presenting the members of your body to sin as instruments of unrighteousness; but present yourselves to God as those alive from the dead, and your members as instruments of righteousness to God" (Romans 6:12,13).

For instance, you can't commit a sexual sin and not use your body as an instrument of unrighteousness. If you do commit a sexual sin, you will allow sin to reign (rule) *in* your mortal body. The only way that we know how to help people get out of sexual bondage is to have them renounce (turn their back on) every sexual use of their body and then commit it to the Lord.

We are dead to sin, but we still have the capacity to serve it by putting our bodies at sin's disposal. It's up to us to choose whether we're going to let our bodies be used for sin or for righteousness. To illustrate, suppose your youth pastor asks to use your car to deliver food baskets to the needy. Moments later a drug dealer asks to use your car to pick up one of his drug shipments. It's your car and you can choose to lend it however you want, for good or for evil. Which would you choose? There should be no question!

Your body is yours to use to serve either God or sin and Satan, but the choice is up to you. That's why Paul wrote so insistently: "I plead with you to give your bodies to God. Let them be a living sacrifice, holy— the kind he can accept. When you think of what He has done for you, is this too much to ask?" (Romans 12:1 TLB).

Because of Christ's victory over sin, you can choose not to obey sin as your master. It is your responsibility not to let sin rule in your body.

You Can Be Free
from the Power of Sin

"Not allowing sin to rule my body sounds wonderful, Neil and Dave," you may be thinking. "But you don't know how hard my battle with sin is. I find myself doing what I shouldn't do and not doing what I should do. It's a constant struggle."

Yes, we know how hard the battle with sin is. So did the apostle Paul. He wrote Romans 7:15-25 out of the same feelings of frustration that you may be experiencing. In this passage we discover God's path to freedom from the power of sin.

Romans 7:15 says: "I don't understand myself at all, for I really want to do what is right, but I can't. I do what I don't want to—what I hate" (TLB). Would you say that this verse describes you—if not always, at least sometimes? Many young Christians desire to do what God says is right, but often find themselves doing just the opposite.

You probably identify with verse 16 as well: "But if I do the very thing I do not wish to do, I agree with the Law, confessing that it is good." It is very defeating when we know what we want to do, but for some reason can't do it. But notice that this person has a good heart, not a bad heart. A non-Christian doesn't confess that the Law is good.

Verses 17 and 18 reveal the cause of the struggle: "So now, no longer am I the one doing it, but sin which indwells me. For I know that nothing good dwells in me, that is, in my flesh." The reason we can't always obey God like we want to is because we have sin—or "nothing good"—dwelling in us. These verses don't say that *we* are no good. They say that *what's dwelling in us*—sin—is no good. If you had a wood splinter in your finger, it would be "nothing good" dwelling in you. But the "nothing good" isn't you; it's the splinter.

We all were born under the *penalty* of sin, and Satan and his demons are always working to keep us under that penalty. When God saved us, Satan lost that battle, but he didn't curl up his tail or pull in his fangs. He is now committed to keep us under the *power* of sin. He works through our flesh, that old pattern of living independently of God, which remained after salvation.

In Romans 7:19-21 we learn more about how this battle is being waged: "For the good that I wish, I do not do; but I practice the very evil I do not wish. But if I am doing the very thing that I do not wish, I am no longer the one doing it, but sin which dwells in me. I find then the principle that evil is present in me, the one who wishes to do good."

From these verses, the "nothing good" that indwells us is clearly evil and sin. There is no question that we sin. Sin is present in us, but we are not sin. This does not excuse us from sinning, because Paul wrote earlier that it is our responsibility not to let sin rule in our bodies (Romans 6:12).

Do you ever feel so defeated in your battle against sin that you want to blame yourself? Then when you cool down, do you again entertain thoughts that are in line with your identity as·a Christian? Sure you do! Verse 22 explains this cycle: "I love to do God's will so far as my new nature is concerned" (TLB). When we act out of character with who we really are, the Holy Spirit immediately brings conviction because of our relationship with God, and we often take it out on ourselves. But soon our true nature expresses itself again and we are drawn back to God.

It's like the frustrated teenager who announces that he's running away from home. He wants out and couldn't care less about how Mom and Dad feel. But after he gets in touch with his pain and expresses his emotions, he softens and says, "I really love my parents, and I don't want to run away. But I just don't see any other way out." That's his true self talking.

Verse 23 describes the nature of this battle with sin: "But I see a different law in the members of my body, waging war against the law of my mind, and making me a prisoner of the law of sin which is in my members." According to this verse, where is the battle being fought? It's in our mind. If Satan can get you to think you are the only one in the battle, you will get down on either yourself or God when you sin.

Let's put it this way: If a dog came along and bit you on the leg, would you beat on yourself or beat on the dog? On the dog of course! But in our struggle with sin, many Christians don't realize that it's the "dog"— sin—that is inflicting the pain! So we beat on ourselves. People eventually get tired of beating on themselves, so they walk away from God under a cloud of defeat and condemnation.

Paul expressed this feeling in verse 24: "Wretched man that I am! Who will set me free from the body of this death?" He's not saying "*wicked* man that I am"; he's saying "*miserable* man that I am." He is defeated because he is not free. His attempts to do the right thing are met with defeat. He wonders, "Is there any victory?"

Verse 25 gives the answer: "Thanks be to God through Jesus Christ our Lord! So then, on the one hand I myself with my mind am serving the law of God, but on the other, with my flesh the law of sin."

If you have been condemning yourself for your inability to live the Christian life, understand that Paul struggled too. Paul was frustrated about his failure, but he didn't get down on himself. He accepted his responsibility, but he didn't condemn himself. More important, he expressed confidence by turning to God, because the Lord Jesus would enable him to live above sin.

Punishing yourself when you sin won't help because there is no condemnation for those who are in Christ Jesus (Romans 8:1,2). You need to understand the nature of the battle for your mind, then discover where you are losing that battle in your own life by allowing sin to rule in your body. When you discover it and deal with it, you can find freedom in Christ.

You Can Win the Battle for Your Mind

Romans 7:23 and 8:5-7 shows that the center of all spiritual bondage is the mind. That's where the battle must be fought and won if we are to experience the freedom in Christ which is our inheritance. Paul wrote: "For though we walk in the flesh, we do not war according to the flesh, for the weapons of our warfare are not of the flesh, but divinely powerful for the destruction of fortresses. We are destroying speculations and every lofty thing raised up against the knowledge of God, and we are taking every thought captive to the obedience of Christ" (2 Corinthians 10:3-5).

Some fortresses (also called "strongholds") of bad habits and sinful thought patterns were established when we learned to live our life independently of God. Our non-Christian environment taught us to think about and respond to life in a non-Christian way, and those patterns and responses were ingrained in our mind as strongholds.

But when we became Christians, nobody pressed the "DELETE" button in our mind. Our old fleshly habits and patterns weren't erased; they are still a part of our flesh which must be dealt with on a daily basis. Thankfully, however, we are not just a product of our past. We are new creatures in Christ (2 Corinthians 5:17), and now we are primarily the product of the work of Christ on the cross. Old strongholds can be destroyed, as outlined in Part Three of this book.

You are now a Christian, but Satan is still interested in using you for his purposes by trying to control your mind. Satan is always trying to promote his lies and to fill your thoughts with his thoughts. He knows that if he can control your thoughts, he can control your behavior.

But Satan is clever. He doesn't rumble in like a bull in a china shop; he slithers in like a snake in the grass (2 Corinthians 11:3). He can introduce his thoughts, tempting you to act independently of God, as if they were your own thoughts or even God's thoughts. Scripture clearly teaches that Satan can put thoughts in our minds even as he did with David (1 Chronicles 21:1), Judas (John 13:2), and Ananias (Acts 5:3).

A student named Jay had an experience that really shows how deceptive Satan's thoughts can be. Jay came into my office one day and said, "Dr. Anderson, I'm in trouble."

"What's the problem, Jay?"

"When I sit down to study I get prickly sensations all over my body, my vision gets blurry, and I can't concentrate."

"Tell me about your walk with God," I probed.

"I have a very close walk with God," Jay boasted.

"What do you mean?"

"Well, when I leave school at noon each day, I ask God where He wants me to go for lunch. If I hear a thought that says, 'Burger King,' I go to Burger King. Then I ask Him what He wants me to eat. If the thought comes to order a Whopper, I order a Whopper."

"What about your church attendance?" I continued.

"I go every Sunday wherever God tells me to go. And for the last three Sundays God has told me to go to a Mormon church."

I immediately knew Satan was invading Jay's thoughts because God would never direct a Christian to a church with a twisted doctrine of Christ and God's Word.

Jay sincerely wanted to do what God wanted him to do. But he was listening to his thoughts as if they were God's voice instead of "taking every thought captive to the obedience of Christ" (2 Corinthians 10:5). He had opened himself up to Satan's schemes in his life.

If you don't conquer Satan's temptation right at the threshold of your mind, you will begin to mull his thoughts over, consider the temptation as an option, and eventually choose to act it out. Repeated acts form a habit, and if you exercise a sinful habit long enough, a stronghold will be established in your mind. Once a stronghold is established you will struggle with the defeated patterns of behavior that Paul described in Romans 7. Much more will be said about Satan's tricks of temptation and his attempts to control our mind and behavior in Part Two.

How are strongholds destroyed? Patterns of sinful thinking and behavior are learned, and they can be unlearned through disciplined Bible study and counseling. Some strongholds are the result of demonic influences and spiritual problems from the past. People with these problems need to be freed from the chains of Satan's lies by God's truth. Jesus said: "You shall know the truth, and the truth shall make you free" (John 8:32). Part Three focuses on the steps to freedom based on the truth of God's Word.

When Morgan, a young Christian girl, came to see me (Dave), she was in bondage to a self-destructive eating disorder. Morgan was the only Christian in her family, and she struggled with insecurity and feelings of being unloved. She was caught in a vicious cycle of overeat-vomit-confess-overeat-vomit-confess. Day after day she lived this nightmare.

My wife, Grace, and I met with her for six hours one day, leading her through the steps to freedom discussed in Part Three. When she left she was a different girl. She no longer needed to beat on herself for the sin and evil that prompted her sick behavior.

Shortly after our meeting with Morgan we received the following letter:

Dear Dave and Grace,

I found myself overeating late this afternoon. Why? Because I was tired. When I'm tired I pressure myself over the edge to do more work, so I overeat. I prayed for God's forgiveness. Thoughts that I should throw up raced into my mind. I was alone. I could have done it. But God would not be glorified if I did that.

Here are the thoughts I allowed into my mind: 1) I'm tired. 2) Satan, you are a rotten liar. 3) God, my body is Your temple. 4) I have been bought with a price; I'm not my own. 5) I could be glorifying God in some other way, not vomiting to make myself feel better. 6) I have people in my life who love me. 7) I don't have to punish myself anymore. 8) I am not bad; in fact, I am righteous. 9) As a precious child of God I will not harm my body or my spirit or my mind with the destruction I cause in my body when I throw up.

I'm laughing now. It feels so good to be in control of myself. This is freedom in Christ.

> Love in Christ,
> Morgan

We hope you're sensing the fact that victory is truly available for those who are in Christ. There is a war raging, but we are on the winning side, for we are more than conquerors in Christ!

Truth Encounter

Read: Romans 7:15-25

Reflect: 1. How will seeing yourself as a saint instead of a sinner have a powerful and positive effect on your daily victory over sin and Satan?

2. In what ways were we trained to live independently of God before we met Christ? How do we overcome those old urges to serve ourselves and learn how to serve God?

3. Why won't punishing yourself for the sins you commit help you overcome them?

4. Repeated acts form habits. How are bad habits or strongholds destroyed?

Respond: Pray and ask the Lord to reveal to your mind any strongholds or bad habits that you might have. Turn to the "Who Am I?" list on page 220 and read through it out loud and carefully.

4
Confronting the Rebel Prince

One of the first persons I (Neil) dealt with about spiritual conflicts and demonic influences was Daisy. She was a Christian with severe mental and emotional problems which developed after her father divorced her mother. Within a period of five years Daisy had been admitted to a mental hospital three times. After about three weeks of counseling with me, Daisy finally found the nerve to bring up the snakes in her life.

"What about the snakes?" I asked.

"Well, they crawl on me at night when I'm in bed," she confessed.

"What do you do when the snakes come?"

"I run in to my mother. But they always come back when I'm alone."

"I'll tell you what you should do," I continued. "When you're in bed and the snakes come, say out loud, 'In the name of Christ I command you to leave me.'"

"I couldn't do that," Daisy protested. "I'm not mature enough or strong enough."

"It's not a matter of your maturity; it's a matter of your position in Christ. You have as much right to resist Satan and make him leave as I do."

Daisy squirmed at the prospect. "Well, I guess I could do that," she sighed, sounding like she had just agreed to take castor oil.

The next week when Daisy walked in she said, "The snakes are gone!"

"Great! Why didn't you tell me about them sooner?"

"Because I was afraid you would get them too. Now I realize that this was just another part of Satan's lie."

Within a few months Daisy was free of the devil's trap and was ministering in our children's department at church.

Before we talk about the reality and present activity of Satan and his demons, you need to understand your position of authority in Christ over the powers of darkness. James wrote: "Resist the devil and he will flee from you" (James 4:7). But if you don't resist him, he doesn't have to go. Or if you just pull the covers over your head in fear and say, "O God, do something about these demonic influences," the evil spirits don't have to leave. Resisting the devil in your life is your responsibility based on the authority you possess in Christ.

Carrying Jesus' Badge of Authority

When Jesus equipped His disciples for ministry, "He called the twelve together, and gave them power and authority over all the demons, and to heal diseases. And He sent them out to proclaim the kingdom of God, and to perform healing" (Luke 9:1,2). Jesus knew that when His disciples began preaching and healing the sick, demonic powers would try to stop them. So He gave them power and authority over demons.

Later Jesus sent out 70 of His followers on a similar mission, and "they returned with joy, saying, 'Lord, even the demons are subject to us in Your name'" (Luke 10:17). They were astonished at the victory they experienced over evil spirits.

But Jesus quickly reminded them that there was something even more important than their authority over evil powers: "I have given you authority over all the power of the Enemy.... However, the important thing is not that demons obey you, but that your names are registered as citizens in heaven" (Luke 10:19,20 TLB). Jesus was saying, don't be demon-centered; be God-centered.

That's a good warning for us. As we learn to use our authority over the kingdom of darkness, we may be tempted to spend all our time studying about Satanism, the occult, and the New Age movement and looking for demons behind every door. But it's the *truth* that sets us free, not how much we know about the lies of Satan. We would have no authority at all if it weren't for our identity as children of God and our position in Christ. *Who we are* is always more important than *what we do*.

The Right and the Ability

Jesus gave His disciples both *authority* and *power*

over demons. What's the difference? Authority is the *right* to rule. For example, a policeman has the right to stop traffic at an intersection because of the position of authority represented by his badge. In the same way, Jesus gave His disciples His badge to carry. They had the right to rule over the demons because of their position as followers of the One to whom all authority in heaven and on earth has been given (Matthew 28:18).

Power is the *ability* to rule. A policeman has the authority to stop traffic, but he doesn't have the physical ability to do so. If he tries to stop traffic by his own power, he will probably get run over. However, if you move a 20-foot-square cement block into the middle of the intersection, it may not have any authority to make cars stop, but it certainly has the ability to do the job!

Jesus gave His followers the *responsibility* of proclaiming the good news, and He also gave them the tools they needed to do the job. If Jesus had not given them both *authority* and *power* in the spirit world, the demons would have just laughed at their feeble attempts and sent them running for cover.

You may think, as Daisy did, that you're not mature enough to resist demons who try to interfere in your life. You say, "After all, I'm just a teenager. The devil is more powerful than I am."

By yourself you don't have the ability to resist Satan and his demons. But *in Christ you do*. In the story of David and Goliath, the Israelites looked at the giant fearfully and said, "We can't fight him." But young David, probably just a teenager, looked at Goliath and said, "Who is this . . . Philistine, that he should taunt the armies of the living God?" (1 Samuel 17:26). Then David blew him away with his slingshot.

The army saw Goliath in relation to themselves and trembled; David saw Goliath in relation to God and triumphed. When you encounter the spiritual enemies of your soul, remember: You plus Jesus equals a majority. A little child, an aged grandmother, or a teenager in Christ have the same authority in the spiritual world as an experienced pastor. We are to "glory in Christ Jesus and put no confidence in the flesh" (Philippians 3:3).

Pulling Rank

It was an eye-opening experience for the disciples to discover that "the demons are subject to us in Your name" (Luke 10:17). This verse pictures a group of soldiers snapping to attention and following precisely the orders of their commanding officer. Jesus was telling us that the demons are the soldiers and, in Christ, we are the generals. They must do what we command in Christ's name.

We sometimes mistakenly see God and His kingdom on one side and Satan and his kingdom on the other side. Both kingdoms seem to be very powerful, and here we are, stuck in the middle between the two, like the rope in a tug-of-war. On some days God seems to be winning, and on other days the devil appears to have the upper hand. And we don't seem to have anything to say about who wins the battle.

But that's not how it is. Spiritual authority is not a tug-of-war; it's a chain of command. Jesus Christ has all authority in heaven and on earth (Matthew 28:18); He's at the top. He has given His authority and power to His children to be used in His name (Luke 10:17); we're underneath Him. What about Satan and his demons? They're at the bottom, subject to the authority Christ has given to us. They have no more right to rule our lives than an army private has to order a general to clean the latrine.

So why does the kingdom of darkness exercise such a powerful evil influence in the world and in the lives of so many young Christians? Because the devil is an excellent liar. Satan's power is not equal with God's; Satan has been totally defeated. But if he can deceive you into believing that he has more power and authority than you do, you will live as if he does! You have been given authority over the kingdom of darkness, but if you don't believe it and use it, it's as if you don't have it.

Jesus' Badge of Authority in Today's World

Christians today enjoy the same claim to Christ's authority in the spiritual world as the disciples who were personally sent out by Him. In fact, because of the death, resurrection, and ascension of Christ, and the outpouring of the Holy Spirit, we have an even greater advantage in spiritual warfare than the first disciples did. They were *with* Christ (Mark 3:14,15), but we are *in* Christ.

That was Paul's great news in the opening lines of Ephesians. Notice how many times he mentions our position in Christ (emphasis added):

> Blessed be the God and Father of our Lord Jesus Christ, who has blessed us with every spiritual blessing in the heavenly places *in Christ*, just as He chose us *in Him*

before the foundation of the world (verses 3,4)....To the praise of the glory of His grace, which He freely bestowed on us *in the Beloved*. *In Him* we have redemption through His blood (verses 6,7)....*In Him* also we have obtained an inheritance...to the end that we who were the first to hope *in Christ* should be to the praise of His glory. *In Him*, you also...were sealed *in Him* with the Holy Spirit of promise (verses 10-13).

Paul wanted to make sure that nobody missed his point. Everything we have is because of our personal relationship with Christ and His indwelling Spirit.

Having firmly established the reality of our position in Christ, Paul expressed his heart's desire for Spirit-controlled believers in this prayer:

I pray that the eyes of your heart may be enlightened, so that you may know what is the hope of His calling, what are the riches of the glory of His inheritance in the saints, and what is the surpassing greatness of His power toward us who believe. These are in accordance with the working of the strength of His might which He brought about in Christ, when He raised Him from the dead, and seated Him at His right hand in heavenly places (Ephesians 1:18-20).

We need our inner eyes opened because our problem is not that we aren't in Christ; it's that we don't *see* it or *understand* it. And when we don't understand who we are, we don't experience the freedom and fruitfulness that goes along with our position in Christ.

Also, Paul suggests that our problem with authority in the spiritual world is not that we aren't tapped into the surpassing greatness of Christ's power; it's that we just don't see it. And as long as we fail to see that Christ's authority is available to us, we will fail to exercise that authority in our lives, and we will live in bondage.

The reason Christ gave us His authority was to demonstrate to the kingdom of darkness who is really in control in this world. In Ephesians 3:8-10, Paul wrote: "To me, the very least of all saints, this grace was given, to preach to the Gentiles the unfathomable riches of Christ . . . in order that the manifold wisdom of God might now be made known through the church to the rulers and authorities in the heavenly places." "Heavenly places" is not a physical place; it is a spiritual realm.

How are we doing at making Christ's victory known to "the rulers and authorities in heavenly places"? In most youth groups, not very well. Some of us are still saying, "What rulers and authorities?" We're not sure that demons even exist. How are we ever going to get our job done in the world if we don't believe what God says about the kingdom of darkness?

Others of us are hiding in a corner pleading, "O God, please help us! The devil is roaring at us!" And God responds, "I've done all I'm going to do. I defeated and disarmed Satan at the cross. I gave you all the authority you need in Christ. Now open your eyes. Realize who you are and assume your responsibility with the authority you already have."

Do You Have
What It Takes?

How do we appropriate Christ's authority over spiritual powers? Does every Christian have this authority regardless of age or level of spiritual maturity? Yes, every believer has spiritual authority because of his or her position in Christ. But there are at least four qualifications for exercising authority over rulers and authorities in the spiritual world.

1. *Belief.* Imagine a rookie traffic cop approaching a busy intersection to direct traffic for the first time. They told him at the academy that all he had to do was step into the street and hold up his hand and the cars would stop, but he's not so sure. He stands on the curb, tweets his whistle weakly, and sort of waves at an oncoming car, which just roars by him. His authority is limited by his lack of confidence.

Now imagine a veteran officer coming on the scene. He sizes up the situation, steps into the street carefully but confidently, gives a blast on his whistle, and stretches out his hand—and the cars stop. There's no doubt in his mind that he's in control in that intersection because he has a settled belief in his authority.

As a Christian, if you don't believe you have authority, you're not going to exercise it. If your belief is weak, your expression of it will also be weak and ineffective. But if you have a confident grip on the authority that Christ has given you, you will exercise it with confidence.

I (Neil) received an interesting phone call one night from a youth pastor whose belief in his authority was being put to the test. He was visiting at the home of one of his young people while the parents were out bowling. It was a Christian family, but an older brother in the home had been living a lie. He was deceiving his family members and being deceived.

"Dr. Anderson, I was sitting here visiting with the kid from my group and his little sister when we sensed an evil presence in the room. It scared us all. I knew something was very wrong."

"What did you do?" I asked.

"I said out loud, 'All right, I know you're here. Show yourself to us.' Suddenly a picture on the wall turned 90 degrees. That's when I decided to call you."

My young friend's belief in his authority had suddenly worn thin. If you ever challenge an evil spirit like he did, you need to be able to exercise your authority in Christ and resolve the conflict.

I went to the house the next night and met with the whole family, including the boy whose lying ways had opened the door for demonic activity. We prayed together, and the father, as head of the household, took authority over their home and committed it and his family to the Lord.

For two days there was no evidence of an evil presence. Then one night the enemy apparently decided to test the family's authority. The little girl woke up in the middle of the night terrified. She saw an eerie light in the hallway shining under her bedroom door. Her parents were asleep across the hall and she wanted to go to them, but she was afraid to open the door. Finally, remembering our prayer time a few nights earlier, she exercised her belief and opened the door. As soon as she did the light was gone, never to return.

You may consider yourself just a "rookie" at stopping the devil's traffic in your life. But Jesus Christ is a seasoned veteran, and you're in Him. Build your faith in your authority by studying how Jesus operated against the powers of darkness in the Gospels and how we are commanded to do so in the Epistles.

2. *Humility.* Humility doesn't mean that you're always looking for a rock to crawl under because you feel unworthy to do anything. Humility is confidence which is properly placed. In exercising our authority, humility is placing confidence in Christ, the source of our authority, instead of in ourselves. Jesus didn't shrink back from exercising His authority, but He showed tremendous humility because He did everything according to what His Father told Him to do.

Pride says, "I resisted the devil all by myself." False humility says, "God resisted the devil; I did nothing." True humility says, "I resisted the devil by the grace of God." Apart from Christ we can do *nothing* (John 15:5), but that doesn't mean we're not supposed to do *something.* We exercise authority humbly in His strength and in His name.

3. *Boldness.* A Spirit-controlled Christian has a true, godly sense of courage and boldness in spiritual warfare. Just before entering the Promised Land, Joshua was challenged four times to be strong and courageous (Joshua 1:6,7,9,18). When the early church prayed about their mission of sharing the gospel in Jerusalem, "the place where they had gathered together was shaken, and they were all filled with the Holy Spirit, and began to speak the word of God with boldness" (Acts 4:31). Spirit-inspired boldness is behind every successful advance in the church today.

The opposite of boldness is cowardice, fear, and unbelief. Notice what God thinks about these characteristics:

> I am the Alpha and Omega, the beginning and the end. I will give to the one who thirsts from the spring of the water of life without cost. He who overcomes shall inherit these things, and I will be his God and he will be My son. But for the cowardly and unbelieving and abominable and murderers and immoral persons and sorcerers and idolaters and all liars, their part will be in the lake that burns with fire and brimstone, which is the second death (Revelation 21:6-8).

That's pretty serious—the cowardly and unbelieving lined up at the lake of fire alongside murderers, sorcerers, and idolaters! It should serve to motivate us to believe God and boldly live a righteous life: "God has not given us a spirit of timidity, but of power and love and discipline" (2 Timothy 1:7).

A lot of Christians fear the dark side of the spiritual world. They say, "I'm afraid to talk about demons." It's true that a little knowledge can be a dangerous and frightful thing, but a growing knowledge of the truth is liberating.

4. *Dependence.* The authority we're talking about here is not an independent authority. We don't charge out on our own like some kind of Christian ghostbusters to hunt down the devil and engage him in combat. God's primary call is for each of us to focus

on the ministry of the kingdom: loving, caring, preaching, teaching, praying, etc. However, when demonic powers challenge us in the course of pursuing this ministry, we deal with them on the basis of our authority in Christ and our dependence on Him. This authority is not over each other for we are to "be subject to one another in the fear of Christ" (Ephesians 5:21). It is over the kingdom of darkness. Light dispels darkness. Truth exposes the lie.

The Bottom Line: Freedom

When we boldly and humbly exercise the authority that Christ has given us over spiritual powers, we experience the freedom from bondage which Christ promised (John 8:32). It's usually a freedom that secular counseling can't produce, as a counselor named Barry discovered.

Christy, a young woman, came to my (Neil) friend Barry because of the horrible abuse she suffered growing up. Barry dealt with Christy's problems with her family and friends, and Christy followed his suggestions. But she didn't get any better. After working with Christy for nearly four years, Barry brought her to me.

"Tell me about your childhood friends, Christy," I probed.

"The only other girl on our block lived across the street from me, so we were friends."

"What was her family like?"

Christy lowered her eyes. "Her mother did strange things in their home," she almost whispered.

"Did these strange things involve candles and sacrifices, sometimes even killing animals?"

"Yeah."

By this time Barry's eyes were as big as silver dollars. In nearly four years of counseling Christy had never told him that a witch lived across the street from her as a child.

"Were you ever required to take off your clothes during these rituals?" Christy nodded. "And were there others there, men and women, who took off their clothes and performed sexual acts with you and each other?" Again she nodded.

Christy's neighbor finally moved away. But every night a demonic manifestation of this witch appeared to her in her room and talked with her. I led Christy through the steps to freedom, and she exercised her authority in Christ and dismissed the evil influence from her life. It came back occasionally, and sometimes Christy failed to stand against it because she was "just tired of fighting the battle." But when she stood her ground on Christ's authority, she was free.

Satan can do nothing about your position in Christ. But if he can, he will cloud your beliefs and confuse you, trying to make you forget who you are in Christ. This is how he tears down your faith and defeats you in spiritual battle.

We want to echo Paul's prayer in Ephesians 1. We pray that your eyes will be opened so you can see and understand the authority and power that Christ has extended to you as a believer.

Truth Encounter

Read: Matthew 28:18; Luke 10:17

Reflect: 1. Jesus gave His followers power and authority over demonic forces. What's the difference between power and authority?

2. Do teenage Christians have the same authority and power over the demonic as the first followers of Jesus?

3. What four qualities need to be present in our lives to make God's authority available to us?

4. Since Satan can do nothing about our position in Christ, how will he try to defeat us in spiritual battle?

Respond: Pray that your eyes will be opened so that you can see and understand the power and authority that Christ has extended to you.

5

Jesus Has You Covered

Have you ever said to yourself, "I've had more trouble in my life since I became a Christian"? A lot of Christians have made that discovery. Why is being a Christian sometimes so tough? Because when we became God's children, we gained an enemy we didn't have before. In our B.C. days (before Christ), the devil didn't bother with us because we were already part of his kingdom. His goal was to keep us there by blinding us to God's plan of salvation (2 Corinthians 4:3,4).

But when we came to life in Christ, Satan didn't curl up his tail and pull in his fangs. He is still committed to fouling up our life with his lies to "prove" that Christianity doesn't work, that God's Word isn't true, and that nothing really happened when we were born again.

"So what's the benefit of being a Christian? Who in his right mind would want to sign up for a life of trouble?" you may wonder. In reality, it doesn't need to be a life of trouble. We don't have to be a defenseless hockey puck at the mercy of Satan and his demons. God has already supplied the protection we need to ward off any and every satanic attack. We just need to know what God has provided and apply it in our own lives.

Some young Christians are a little paranoid about evil powers. They fear that demons are waiting around every corner to possess them. That's an unreal fear. Our relationship to demonic powers in the spiritual world is a lot like our relationship to germs in the physical world. We know that germs are all around us: in the air, in the water, in our food, in other people, even in us. But do we live in constant fear of catching some disease? No—unless you're a hypochondriac! We should know enough about healthy living to eat the right foods, get enough rest, and keep ourselves clean. Don't be germ conscious. Be health conscious and your immune system will protect you. If we happen to catch a cold or get the measles, we simply deal with it and go on with our life.

It's the same in the spiritual world. Demons are like little invisible germs looking for someone to infect. We are never told in the Bible to be afraid of them. We just need to be aware that they are real and commit ourselves to live a righteous life in spite of them. Should we come under attack, we deal with it and go on with life. Don't be demon-centered; be Christ-centered.

Remember: The only thing big about a demon is its mouth. Demons are habitual liars. In Jesus Christ the Truth, we are equipped with all the authority and protection we need to deal with anything they throw at us.

Getting Involved in
God's Protection

Ephesians 6:10-18 tells us all about God's protection program. Notice how often we are commanded to be actively involved in the spiritual defense that He has provided for us:

> Finally, *be strong* in the Lord, and in the strength of His might. *Put on* the full armor of God, that you may *be able* to *stand firm* against the schemes of the devil. For our struggle is not against flesh and blood, but against the rulers, against the powers, against the world forces of this darkness, against the spiritual forces of wickedness in the heavenly places. Therefore, *take up* the full armor of God, that you may *be able* to *resist* in the evil day, and having done everything, to *stand firm* (verses 10-13, emphasis added).

You may be wondering, "If my position in Christ is secure and my protection is found in Him, why do I have to get involved? Can't I just kick back and let Him protect me?"

That's like a soldier saying, "Our country has a big, powerful army. We have the most advanced tanks and planes in the world. Why should I bother with wearing a helmet or learning to shoot a gun? I'll just stay in camp while the tanks and planes fight the war." When the enemy troops appear, guess which soldier will get shot first!

God, our "commanding officer," has provided everything we need to win the battle against the evil forces of darkness. But He says, "I've prepared a winning battle plan and designed effective weapons. But if you don't do your part by staying on active duty, you're likely to become a casualty." You can't expect God to protect you from demonic influences if you don't take an active part in His prepared strategy.

Dressed for Success

The armor that God has provided for us and instructed us to wear is our main protection from the enemy. Paul wrote:

> Stand firm then, with the belt of truth buckled around your waist, with the breastplate of righteousness in place, and with your feet fitted with the readiness that comes from the gospel of peace. In addition to all this, take up the shield of faith, with which you can extinguish all the flaming arrows of the evil one. Take the helmet of salvation and the sword of the Spirit, which is the word of God (Ephesians 6:14-17 NIV).

When we put on the armor of God we are really putting on Christ (Romans 13:12-14). And when we put on Christ we put ourselves under Christ's protection where the evil one cannot touch us (1 John 5:18).

Armor You Have Already Put On

It appears from Ephesians 6:14,15 that we are already wearing three of the pieces of armor: the belt, breastplate, and shoes. These pieces of armor represent the protection given to us when we received Jesus

Christ. We are not commanded to put these pieces on but to stand firm in them.

The belt of truth. Jesus said, "I am the truth" (John 14:6). And because Christ is in us, the truth is in us. However, continuing to choose truth is not always easy. Since Satan's main weapon is the lie, our belt of truth (which holds the other pieces of body armor in place) is continually being attacked. If he can disable us in the area of truth, we become an easy target for his other attacks.

We stand firm in the truth by relating everything we do to the truth of God's Word. If a thought comes to mind that doesn't go along with God's truth, kick it out. If an opportunity comes along to say or do something that compromises or conflicts with truth, avoid it. Adopt a simple rule of behavior: If it's the truth, I'm in; if it's not the truth, count me out.

The breastplate of righteousness. When we put on Christ at salvation we were forgiven, justified, and we became partakers of Christ's divine nature (2 Peter 1:4). It's not *our* righteousness but Christ's (1 Corinthians 1:30; Philippians 2:8,9). So when Satan aims an arrow at you by saying, "You're not good enough to be a Christian," you can respond with Paul, "Who will bring any charge against those whom God has chosen? It is God who justifies" (Romans 8:33 NIV). Your position in Christ is your protection against Satan's accusations that you're nothing but a worthless sinner.

Even though we're happy about our position of righteousness in Christ, we are well aware that we sometimes think, say, or do things we shouldn't. We are saints who sin. Standing firm in our righteousness involves understanding and applying what God's Word says about confession.

God's remedy for sin is stated in 1 John 1:9: "If we confess our sins, He is faithful and righteous to forgive us our sins and to cleanse us from all unrighteousness." Confession is different from saying, "I'm sorry," or asking forgiveness. To confess means to agree with God.

Suppose when you were younger your father caught you throwing a rock at a car. Dad says, "You threw a rock at a car, and that was wrong." If you respond, "I'm sorry, Dad," have you confessed? Not really. You may also say, "Please forgive me, Dad," but have you confessed yet? No. You haven't confessed until you agree with your dad and say, "I threw a rock at a car. I was wrong."

When we sin we may feel sorry, but feeling sorry or even telling God we're sorry isn't confession. We confess our sin when we say what God says about it: "I thought about that girl (or guy) with lust, and that's a sin"; "I yelled at my brother angrily this morning, and that was wrong"; "pride motivated me to seek that student council position, and pride doesn't belong in my life."

Satan will make confession as difficult for you as he can. He will try to convince you that it's too late for confession, that God has already erased your name out of the Book of Life. That's another one of his big lies. You're in Christ; you're already forgiven. You are righteous in Christ (2 Corinthians 5:21), and He will never leave you. Your relationship with God is not at stake when you sin, but your daily victory is. Your confession of sin clears the way for you to live a righteous life day by day.

The shoes of peace. When we receive Christ we are united with the Prince of Peace. We have peace *with* God right now (Romans 5:1), but the peace *of* Christ must also rule in our heart. That is possible only when we fill our heart daily with God's Word (Colossians 3:15,16).

The shoes of peace become protection against the many schemes of the devil when you act as a peacemaker among believers (Romans 14:19). Peacemakers bring people together by promoting fellowship and by bringing divided Christians together. Preserve Christian unity by being a peacemaker in your relationships (Matthew 5:9; Ephesians 4:3).

The Rest of the Wardrobe

Paul mentions three more pieces of armor that we must put on to protect ourselves from Satan's attack: the shield of faith, the helmet of salvation, and the sword of the Spirit, which is the Word of God. The first three pieces of armor are the result of our position in Christ; the last three help us continue to win the battle.

The shield of faith. Faith is simply what you believe about God and His Word. The more you know about God and His Word, the more faith you will have. The less you know, the smaller your shield of faith will be and the easier it will be for one of Satan's fiery arrows to hit you. If you want your shield of faith to grow large and provide greater protection from Satan, you need to increase your knowledge of God and His Word (Romans 10:17).

These flaming arrows from Satan are nothing more than smoldering lies, burning accusations, and fiery temptations bombarding our minds. When a deceptive thought, accusation, or temptation enters your mind, meet it head-on with what you know to be true about God and His Word. How did Jesus deflect Satan's temptation? By shielding Himself with statements from the Word of God. Every time you memorize a Bible verse, listen to a sermon, or participate in a Bible study at youth group, you increase your knowledge of God and enlarge your shield of faith. We are not called to dispel the darkness; we are called to turn on the light. You overcome a lie by choosing the truth.

The helmet of salvation. If your shield of faith is a little leaky and your daily victory difficult to achieve, be confident that the helmet of salvation guarantees your eternal victory. The helmet also covers the most important part of your body: your mind, where spiritual battles are either won or lost. As you struggle with the world, the flesh, and the devil on a daily basis, stand firm knowing that your salvation does not come and go with your success or failure in spiritual battle. You are a child of God, and nothing can separate you from the love of Christ (Romans 8:35).

The sword of the Spirit. The Word of God is the only offensive weapon mentioned in the list of armor. In this verse Paul seems to be referring to the spoken Word of God instead of Jesus Christ, the living Word of God. We are to defend ourselves against the evil one by speaking aloud God's truth.

Why is it so important to speak God's Word in addition to believing it and thinking it? Because Satan doesn't perfectly know what we're thinking. He is a created being; he can't read our thoughts like God can. If we only tell Satan to leave with our thoughts, he may not leave because he can't hear us. *We must defeat Satan by speaking out.*

One night I (Neil) woke up absolutely terrified for no apparent reason. It was a fear that made my skin crawl, and I knew it was an attack from Satan. Without lifting my head from the pillow, I applied the two-step remedy suggested by James: "Submit therefore to God. Resist the devil and he will flee from you" (4:7). In my heart, out of Satan's earshot, I submitted to God by praying, "Lord, I acknowledge Your sovereign grace over my life right now. You are my God." Then I resisted Satan with one spoken word—*Jesus*—and the fear was instantly and totally gone. I went back to sleep in complete peace.

Even my (Dave) three-year-old daughter Dani has learned to send the enemy running by speaking out on the authority of God's Word. After my wife, Grace, and I joined Freedom in Christ Youth Ministries, Dani began sensing an evil presence in her room at night—a creature she called "Ugly Sun" with four others she called monkeys. She knew they were bad and was terrified by their presence.

One night we heard her crying. As we entered her room she said the creatures were there. She was so scared she literally tried to crawl inside Grace's pajamas to hide. We coached Dani in a prayer, and even though she was scared, she repeated after us these simple words: "By the power and the blood of Jesus, all the evil ones must leave."

Then Dani looked up, smiled, and with complete calmness said, "They're gone." She crawled under her covers and was asleep again in just a few minutes.

Age and physical strength have nothing to do with success in spiritual warfare (2 Corinthians 10:4); it is the Lord's strength that sends evil spirits running for cover. The power is in the spoken Word.

The Protective Power of Prayer

One young girl I (Dave) know saw God work in a powerful way through prayer. Mary's parents had been divorced for more than ten years, and her mother was heavily involved in the New Age movement. For as long as she could remember, her parents never had a kind word for each other, and it was breaking her heart. Mary's mother also constantly put her down, telling Mary that she couldn't love her because she was overweight. Mary wasn't even allowed to call her own mother "Mom." She had to call her by her first name. Mary desperately wanted to be loved and accepted by her mother, and for her parents to be kind to each other.

The situation was so bad that Mary was even afraid to pray about it. She figured that it really wasn't fair to ask God to do something so hard. I encouraged Mary that nothing is impossible or too hard for God. We prayed for her mother, that her mind would be a quiet place where God could speak to her and that she would not continue to discourage her daughter.

I received a phone call from Mary a few days after our prayer together. She was so excited she could hardly control herself. "Prayer works! Prayer really works!" she exclaimed. "My mother just called a short time ago and she actually talked to my dad! They were even kind to each other. She then spoke with me, and she said she wanted to just call me up and say how proud she was that I was her daughter and that she loved me. Isn't God awesome? Prayer is powerful!"

One of the most dramatic deliverances I (Neil) have observed happened in a man who was a high priest in Satanism. Six months after he was set free he gave his testimony in our church. At the close of his testimony I asked him, "Based on your experience on 'the other side,' what is the Christian's first line of defense against demonic influence?"

"Prayer," he answered forcefully. "And when you pray, mean it. Fervent prayer blocks Satan's activity like nothing else."

We never know completely the effects of our prayers. But we do know that God includes our prayer as part of His strategy for establishing His kingdom. After instructing us to put on the armor that God has provided, Paul wrote: "Pray all the time. Ask God for anything in line with the Holy Spirit's wishes. Plead with him, remind him of your needs, and keep praying earnestly for the Christians everywhere" (Ephesians 6:18 TLB).

What is prayer? It is communication with God by which we tell Him we are depending on Him. God knows what we need in our battle with the powers of darkness, and He is more ready to meet our needs than we are to ask. But until we express our dependence on Him in prayer, God will not act.

In prayer we say, "You are the Lord, not I. You know what's best; I don't. I'm not telling You what to do; I'm asking. I declare my dependence on You." Our prayers open the way for God to act for us.

Praying for Spiritual Sight

There are several specific needs we should pray about in spiritual warfare. One target of our prayers is the blindness Satan has caused in unbelievers (2 Corinthians 4:3,4). People cannot come to Christ unless their spiritual eyes are opened.

Prayer is a primary weapon in combating spiritual blindness. The apostle John wrote: "If we ask anything according to His will, He hears us. And if we know that He hears us in whatever we ask, we know that we have the requests which we have asked from Him" (1 John 5:14,15). Then he immediately challenged believers to apply what they learned by asking God to bring life to unbelievers (verse 16). Our strategy for bringing others to Christ must include prayer that God's light would penetrate Satan's blindness.

We also need to pray, as Paul did in Ephesians 1:18,19, that the eyes of believers may be opened to understand our spiritual power, authority, and protection in Christ. As long as Satan can keep us in the dark about our position and authority in Christ, our growth, witness, and service as Christians will be severely limited. We need to pray for each other continually that Satan's smokescreen of lies will be blown away and that our vision into the spiritual world will be crystal-clear.

Binding the Strong Man

Another target for prayer is the "strong man" talked about in Matthew 12:29. Jesus said, referring to

Satan and his demons: "How can anyone enter the strong man's house and carry off his property, unless he first binds the strong man?" He was saying that you can't rescue people from the chains of spiritual blindness or demonic influence unless you first overpower their captors. Satan's power is already broken, but he won't let go of anything until we exercise our authority in Christ.

When we pray against the strong man, we grab onto what rightfully belongs to God and hold on until Satan turns loose. He will hold onto these people until we demand their release on the basis of our authority in Christ. Once Satan is bound through prayer, he must let go.

Several years ago a personal experience emphasized to me (Neil) the power of prayer in dealing with people who are in the clutches of the strong man. A man named Bill came to my office one Sunday afternoon. I barely knew him, and I didn't have much time to chat. But I was concerned about Bill, so I began, "I'm glad you're here, Bill. May I ask you a personal question?" Bill nodded. "Have you ever trusted in Christ to be your Lord and your Savior?"

"No."

"Would you like to?"

"I don't know, Neil," Bill answered with a slightly troubled expression.

I brought out a salvation tract and read through it with him. "Do you understand this, Bill?"

"Yes."

"Would you like to make that decision for Christ now?"

"Yes."

"I'll pray a simple prayer of commitment, and you repeat it after me phrase by phrase, okay?"

"Okay."

"Lord Jesus, I need you," I began.

Bill began to respond, "Lor-r-r..." Then he locked up completely. I realized that I had invaded the territory of the strong man, Satan, and he didn't want to let go of Bill.

"Bill, there's a battle going on for you," I said. "I'm going to read some Scripture and pray out loud for you. I'm going to bind the enemy and stand against him. As soon as you can, you just tell Jesus what you believe." His eyes told me that the battle within him was raging.

I started reading Scripture and praying aloud every prayer I could think of to bind Satan and set Bill free. After several minutes of prayer and Scripture, Bill suddenly groaned, "Lord Jesus, I need You." Then he slumped back in his chair like he had just gone ten rounds with the world heavyweight champion. He looked at me with tear-filled eyes and said, "I'm free." I had never used the word "freedom" with him; that was his expression. But he was free and he knew it.

God has equipped you with everything you need to ward off the attack of the strong man in your life. And He has also equipped you and authorized you for "search and rescue" in the lives of those who are in the devil's clutches. Stand firm in the armor that God has provided and step out in Christ's authority to rob the strong man's house for God.

Truth Encounter

Read: Ephesians 6:10-18

Reflect: 1. Many young Christians often have more trouble in their lives after they accept Christ than before. Why do you think this might be true?

2. Which of the six pieces of God's armor do you think you need to focus on in your spiritual conflicts at home, school, and with friends?

3. In the midst of a spiritual conflict, have you ever doubted your salvation? Why is it important to understand that your salvation is an eternal possession?

4. What are the two areas of prayer talked about in this chapter? Have you ever prayed for someone regarding these areas? What were the results?

Respond: After reading Ephesians 6:10-18, decide to put on the armor of God. Pray out loud as you put on each piece. Also ask God to reveal to your mind those people you know who are blinded in their unbelief. Make a list of their names as they come to mind and pray for their salvation daily.

PART TWO

Stand Firm!

6

Dealing with Evil in Person

"What in the world happened to Harry?" The woman speaking to me (Neil) over the phone was referring to her former boyfriend. Harry was the satanic high priest I mentioned in the last chapter who found Christ and was set free from unbelievable bondage to darkness. Evelyn told me that she had urged Harry to get out of Satanism. But she never expected the big change which had occurred in him. She wanted some answers.

"I'll be happy to sit down with you and talk about it," I replied. So we set up an appointment at my office.

As she began to tell me about herself, Evelyn mentioned that she was a Christian, but I had my doubts. I casually asked her what her salvation was based on. True to my suspicions, her answers were filled with self-righteous statements. I realized that I was dealing with a very deceived person.

"When Harry and I got together," she continued,

"we would go into a Catholic church and she would speak to Harry there."

"You mean a nun would come and counsel Harry?" I asked.

"No, she would speak to him through me."

Suddenly the light came on. "You're saying that someone inside you was communicating with Harry using your voice, and that this person was a she."

Evelyn nodded. "Not only was she a she, she was Irish."

"Evelyn, the Bible tells us to test the spirits. Did you ever test this spirit?"

"No, I had no reason to."

"Would you be willing to test this spirit now?"

"Sure."

"In the name of Jesus Christ," I prayed, "I bind you to silence, spirit, unless I command you to speak. Now in Christ's name, identify yourself to Evelyn's mind." I wanted Evelyn to tell me what she heard.

A puzzled look came over Evelyn's face. "She says she is Maggie McKendall." What followed was a three-way conversation. I addressed my questions to the spirit in Evelyn. The spirit answered my question by speaking to Evelyn's mind, which she heard as clearly in her head as she heard me with her ears. Then Evelyn told me what she heard.

"How old are you, Maggie McKendall?" I asked.

"Soul life has no age."

"Why did you come?"

"To help the saints in warfare."

"Were you ever alive on planet Earth?"

"Yes."

"When did you die?"

Evelyn relayed the answer that Maggie McKendall died in the 1970s in Ireland.

If you know your Bible, you know that I wasn't talking with a dead Irish Christian named Maggie McKendall who had returned in spirit form to help the saints in warfare. Jesus' account of the rich man and Lazarus in Luke 16:19-31 clearly shows that there is a great, impassable canyon between the living and the dead. No one who crosses from life to death can return. The only Spirit God has sent to help us in warfare is the Holy Spirit.

By that time in the conversation I was sure that I was dealing with a demon who was deceiving Evelyn into believing that it was there to help her. So I continued with a question which I knew would expose the spirit: "Maggie McKendall, is Jesus your Lord?"

"Yes," Evelyn answered for the spirit.

I was really puzzled. Here was a spirit obviously from the kingdom of darkness who was confessing Jesus Christ as its Lord! I have asked numerous other spirits that question. Some of them respond angrily, "No!" Others of them answer, "Yes, Jesus Christ is Lord." But when I press them by asking if Jesus Christ is *their own* Lord, none of them answer yes. Either Evelyn wasn't telling me the truth about what she was hearing or else something was very wrong.

"Did Jesus Christ come in the flesh?" I continued.

Again her answer took me off guard: "Yes."

I was totally baffled that the spirit controlling her claimed Jesus Christ as Lord. I concluded the session quickly and she left.

While I was on my way home it suddenly hit me: I had been deceived too! I hadn't been talking to the spirit; I had been talking to the role that the spirit was playing—that of Maggie McKendall. There likely was an Irish Christian named Maggie McKendall who had died in the 1970s, and the demon in Evelyn was playing that role. As long as I kept questioning Maggie McKendall, the demon was free to answer the way Maggie McKendall would answer: "Yes, Jesus Christ is my Lord."

Now when I encounter a spirit who is trying to impersonate someone from the past, I simply say, "That's a lie; you're an evil spirit." Then, if the person is willing, I lead him or her through the steps to freedom. I have also learned how to avoid talking with evil spirits completely and not to believe anything they say. Jesus warned us in John 8:44: "Whenever he [the devil] speaks a lie, he speaks from his own nature; for he is a liar, and the father of lies."

A Rebel Authority Is in Control

We live in a world which is under the authority of an evil ruler. Originally God created Adam and his race to rule over creation. But Adam gave up his position of authority through sin, and Satan became the rebel holder of authority. Jesus called him "the ruler of this world" (John 12:31; 14:30; 16:11).

Satan ruled from Adam until the cross. The death, resurrection, and ascension of Christ secured forever the final authority for Jesus Himself (Matthew 28:18).

That authority was given to all believers in the Great Commission so that we could continue His work of destroying the works of the devil (1 John 3:8).

The Powers That Be

Most Christians agree that Satan is a living being who is responsible for the evil in the world today. But when you start talking about demons being alive and active in the world today, a lot of Christians resist: "Hold on there. I believe in the devil, but I don't buy that stuff about demons."

Think about it: How does Satan carry on his world-wide ministry of evil and deception? He is a created being. He isn't all-knowing or all-powerful. He can't be everywhere in the world tempting and deceiving millions of people at the same moment. He does it through an army of spiritual beings (demons, evil spirits, fallen angels, etc.) who carry out his plan of rebellion around the world.

Perhaps the best description of the evil spiritual army which harasses God's people is found in Ephesians 6:12: "Our struggle is not against flesh and blood, but against the rulers, against the powers, against the world forces of this darkness, against the spiritual forces of wickedness in the heavenly places." It is clear from the verses surrounding Ephesians 6:12 that the rulers, powers, and forces which oppose us are spiritual beings in the spiritual world.

We have been targeted by demons numerous times. However, it's not a frightening experience for us, and it shouldn't be for you. John promised, "Greater is He who is in you than he who is in the world" (1 John 4:4). You have authority over Satan's activity and you have the armor of God to protect you. Whenever Satan attacks, you must "be strong in the Lord, and in the strength of His might" (Ephesians 6:10). Consciously place yourself in the Lord's hands and resist Satan by speaking God's Word. You are only open to the devil's arrows when you are walking by sight instead of by faith or walking in the flesh instead of in the Spirit.

What should we do about Satan's hierarchy of demonic powers? Nothing! We are not to be demon-centered; we are to be God-centered and ministry-centered. We are to fix our eyes on Jesus, share the gospel, love one another, and be God's ambassadors in our fallen world.

The Personality of Demons

The Bible does not attempt to prove the existence of demons any more than it attempts to prove the existence of God. It simply reports on their activities as if its readers accepted their existence. Nor did the early church leaders have a problem with the reality and personality of demons.

Luke 11:24-26 gives us a helpful view into evil spirits. After Jesus cast out a demon which had made a man unable to speak, His enemies accused Him of casting out demons by the power of "Beelzebul, the ruler of the demons" (Luke 11:15). During the discussion of demons which followed, Jesus said: "When the unclean spirit goes out of a man, it passes through waterless places seeking rest, and not finding any, it says, 'I will return to my house from which I came.' And when it comes, it finds it swept and put in order. Then it goes and takes along seven other spirits more evil than itself, and they go in and live there; and the last state of that man becomes worse than the first" (verses 24-26).

We can learn several things about evil spirits from this passage.

1. *Demons can exist outside or inside humans.* Demons seem to want a home in a living being. A group of them once asked Jesus to send them into a herd of pigs (Mark 5:12). Some spirits apparently stay in certain geographical locations which have been used for satanic purposes. Satan and demons are spirits. In order to rule in the physical world, they need willing subjects to do their bidding. Deceived people are actually doing the work of Satan. God also is spirit (John 4:24) and accomplishes His will on planet Earth by working through the church, His people.

2. *Demons are able to travel at will.* As spiritual beings, demons are not subject to the barriers of the natural world. The walls of your church building do not make it safe from demonic influence; only prayer and spiritual authority can do that.

3. *Demons are able to communicate.* It is obvious from Luke 11 that evil spirits can communicate with each other. They can also speak to humans through a person, such as they did through the demon-possessed man in Mark 5:1-20.

4. *Each demon has a separate identity.* Notice the use of personal pronouns in Luke 11: "I will return to my house from which I came" (verse 24). We are dealing with thinking personalities as opposed to a force. That's why worldly methods of research are not going

to reveal their existence. The Bible alone is our source on the reality and personality of evil spirits.

5. *Demons are able to remember and make plans.* The fact that demons can leave a place, come back, remember what happened earlier, and plan reentry with others shows their ability to think and plan.

6. *Demons are able to evaluate and make decisions.* The fact that the evil spirit found his human target "swept and put in order" (verse 25) shows that it can evaluate its intended victim. Demons gain access to our lives through our points of weakness.

7. *Demons are able to combine forces.* In Luke 11, one spirit joined with a group of seven others, making things far worse for the victim. In Mark 5, so many demons ganged up on one man that he called himself "Legion" (verse 9), which refers to a large group of soldiers.

8. *Demons vary in degrees of wickedness.* The first demon in Luke 11 brought back seven other spirits "more evil than itself" (verse 26). Jesus indicated a difference in the wickedness of spirits when He said of one, "This kind cannot come out by anything but prayer" (Mark 9:29). The idea of differences in power and wickedness fits the levels that Paul lists in Ephesians 6:12.

Dealing with the Evil Around Us

How do these evil spirits interfere with our lives? Here's a simple illustration. Imagine that you are standing at one end of a long, narrow street lined on both sides with two-story houses. At the other end of the street stands Jesus Christ. Your Christian life is the process of walking down that long street of maturity in Him. There is absolutely nothing in the street that can keep you from reaching Jesus. So, when you receive Christ, you fix your eyes on Him and start walking.

But since this world is still under the control of Satan, the rows of houses on either side of the street are filled with beings who are committed to keeping you from reaching your goal. They have no power or authority to block your path or even slow your step. So they hang out of the windows and call to you, hoping to turn your attention away from your goal and disrupt your progress.

One of the ways they will try to distract you is by calling out, "Hey, look over here! I've got something you really want. It tastes good, feels good, and is a lot more fun than your boring walk down the street. Come on in and take a look." That's temptation, suggesting to your mind ways to serve yourself instead of God. We will talk more about temptation in Chapter 8.

As you continue your walk toward Christ you will also have thoughts like "I'm stupid. I'm ugly. I'll never amount to anything for God." Satan's demons are masters at accusation, especially after they have distracted you through temptation. One minute they're saying, "Try this; there's nothing wrong with it." Then, when you give in to temptation, they're right there taunting, "See what you did! How can you call yourself a Christian when you behave like that?" Accusation is one of Satan's primary weapons in his attempt to distract us from our goal. We will talk about his strategy of accusation in Chapter 9.

Other messages which are thrown at you as you walk down the street sound like this: "You don't need to go to youth group today. It's not important to pray and read the Bible every day. Some of the New Age stuff isn't so bad." That's deception, and it is Satan's most powerful and crippling weapon.

The devil will often introduce these messages as if we are thinking them: "*I* don't need to go to youth group today, pray, read my Bible," etc. Satan knows we will be more easily deceived if he can make us think the thought was ours instead of his. Satan's strategy of deception will be talked about in Chapter 10.

What is the enemy's goal in having his demons jeer at you, taunt you, lure you, and question you from the windows and doorways along your path? He wants you to slow down, stop, sit down, and if possible, give up your journey toward Christ. He wants to influence you to doubt your ability to believe and serve God. Remember: He has absolutely no power or authority to keep you from steadily moving forward in your walk toward Christ. And he can never again own you, because you have been redeemed by Jesus Christ and you are forever in Him (1 Peter 1:18,19).

But if he can get you to listen to the thoughts he plants in your mind, he can influence you. And if you allow him to influence you long enough through temptation, accusation, and deception, he can control you. We'll talk more about how much the devil can control a Christian in Chapter 11.

Levels of Bondage

There are several levels of spiritual freedom and bondage. On one side is the apostle Paul, whose

Christian life and ministry were a great example despite his battle with sin and Satan (Romans 7:15-25; 2 Corinthians 12:7-9). On the other side is the man called Legion, who was totally controlled by demons (Mark 5:1-20).

Nobody loses control to Satan overnight; it's a gradual process of being deceived and yielding to his subtle influence. From what we have seen, no more than 15 percent of all Christian youth are completely free of Satan's bondage. These are the kids who are consistently living a Spirit-filled life and bearing fruit. The other 85 percent are struggling along fruitlessly at one of at least three levels of spiritual conflict.

First, a believer may lead a fairly normal Christian life on the outside while wrestling with a steady stream of sinful thoughts on the inside: lust, envy, greed, hatred, apathy, etc. This person has almost no devotional life. Prayer is a frustrating experience for him, and he usually struggles to get along with family and friends.

Most Christians in this condition have no idea that they are in the middle of a spiritual conflict. They might not say they are hearing voices but would quickly admit to problems controlling their thoughts. Instead of recognizing that their minds are being peppered by the fiery arrows of the enemy, they think the problem is their own fault. "If those bad thoughts are mine, what kind of person am I?" they wonder. So they end up condemning themselves while the enemy continues his attack. We estimate that about 65 percent of all Christians are living at this level of spiritual conflict.

The second level of conflict is characterized by those who see a difference between their own thoughts and strange, evil "voices" which seem to overpower them. "What am I thinking?" they wonder with alarm when sinful ideas, thoughts, and fantasies flood their minds. They experience no victory, and they are so afraid they're going crazy that they won't share their problem with anyone.

Yet the majority of Christians at this level fail to see their struggle as a spiritual conflict. They seek counseling and try to control their thoughts, but they experience little or no improvement. We estimate that about 15 percent of all Christians fall into this category. Most of these people are depressed, anxious, paranoid, bitter, or angry, and may be addicted to alcohol, drugs, eating disorders, etc.

At the third level of conflict, the person has lost all control. Voices inside his mind tell him what to think, say, and do. These people stay at home, wander the streets talking to imaginary people, or occupy beds in mental institutions or rehab units. Sadly, about 5 percent of the Christian community falls victim to this level of deception and control.

Just Say No

There are three ways of responding to the temptations, accusations, and deceptions demons throw at us during our daily walk with Christ, and two of these ways are wrong.

First, the most defeated young people are those who listen to demonic thoughts and believe them. An evil spirit whispers to us, "You don't pray, read your Bible, or witness like you should. How could God love you?" That's a huge lie because God's love is unconditional. But they start thinking about their failures and agreeing that they're probably not very lovable to God. Pretty soon they are sitting in the middle of the street going nowhere.

These Christians are totally defeated simply because they have been fooled into believing that God doesn't love them, or that they will never be a victorious Christian, or that they are a helpless victim of the past. There is no reason why they can't get up immediately and start walking again, but they have believed a lie, so they don't go anywhere.

The second response is just as worthless. We try to argue with the demons: "I am not ugly or stupid. I am a victorious Christian." We're proud that we don't believe what they say, but they're still telling us what to think and do. We're standing in the middle of the street shouting at them when we should be marching forward.

We are not to believe evil spirits, nor are we to talk with them. Instead, the right response is to ignore them. We are equipped with the armor of God; evil powers can't touch us unless we drop our guard. With every arrow of temptation, accusation, or deception they shoot at us, we simply raise the shield of faith, deflect the attack, and walk on (Colossians 2:6). Take every thought captive to the obedience of Christ. Choose truth in the face of every lie. As you do, you will find your maturity and freedom increasing with every step.

Truth Encounter

Read: Ephesians 6:12; Luke 11:24-26

Reflect: 1. What are some of the ways young people picture Satan and demons? Do most young people believe that Satan and demons exist? What do you believe?

2. Can evil spirits put tempting thoughts in our minds? What are some of the ways we are tempted or distracted from following Christ?

3. What are some of the deceptive or accusing thoughts Satan might use against us? What deceptions has he placed in your mind?

4. Is it possible for Satan to gain control over a believer? What must be done to stop Satan's influence in our life?

Respond: Nowhere in the Bible are we told to fear evil spirits or Satan. Pray and claim the protection and the authority you have in Christ. Thank God that Satan and his evil followers were defeated through Christ's death, burial, and resurrection. Pray out loud daily, "By the power and the blood of the Lord Jesus Christ I command any and all evil to leave my presence."

7

The Lure of Knowledge and Power

In previous chapters we talked about Harry, the former high priest of Satanism. Now we want to tell you more of Harry's story to illustrate a point of weakness we share with him.

Harry's mother had been a high priestess in Satanism and had prepared him for his secret role in Satan worship. He was involved in hard-core Satanism at a level that very few people ever hear about.

Six months before he came to see me (Neil), Harry had decided to walk away from Satanism. But when he tried, the powers of darkness held onto their prize in a scary way, resulting in violent physical outbursts. His landlady was deeply frightened, so she called the paramedics. The demonic influence held Harry in such bondage that it took seven paramedics to restrain him.

After observing Harry for a day, the doctors couldn't find anything wrong with him and let him go. After several futile attempts to get out of Satanism, Harry finally came to see me.

Once Harry was seated, he said, "You have no idea what kind of power you're up against."

"Yes, I think I *do* understand the power of Satan," I answered calmly. "But you obviously have no idea of the power of God. You say you want to get out of the darkness, but you have discovered that you can't do it on your own. In order to be free you must choose Christ as your Lord; only He can set you free. Are you prepared to choose Christ?"

Harry began to shake a little, and I realized that the enemy wasn't going to give up without a fight. I decided that I needed some additional support for prayer and accountability, so I left Harry in my office while I went to look for someone who could join me. The only person I could find was Wayne, our custodian. Wayne agreed to sit in my office and pray as I dealt with Harry. Wayne was a good Christian man who had served as an elder in our church. But I knew he had never seen anything like what he was about to see!

I sat down facing Harry and said, "Are you prepared to make a decision for Christ, Harry?" He started to squirm a little in his chair. Suddenly he exploded with a roar. Then he stood up and seemed to be thrown across the room. He yelled and screamed and rolled around the office like a crazy man. The demons who controlled Harry were using his mind, his will, his muscles, and his emotions in a noisy display of resistance.

By this time Wayne was plastered against the wall, praying like he had never prayed in his life! But I just sat still. I learned a long time ago that Satan's show of power is just another way to try to make us afraid. He knows that if he can deceive us into being afraid of him, fear will control us instead of faith.

Satan "prowls about like a roaring lion, seeking someone to devour" (1 Peter 5:8). But because of our position, authority, and protection in Christ, Satan can't touch us. Fear is a powerful controller. If you cower in fear at Satan's show of power, he has you on the defensive. But Peter instructed, "Resist him, firm in your faith" (1 Peter 5:9). Satan is defeated; believe it and stand up to him. When you do, he has no choice but to eventually back down.

As the devil roared at me through Harry, I began to read Scripture aloud and pray in a normal, controlled voice that the enemy would be bound in silence. The portion of Scripture I usually read in these encounters is Ephesians 1, which clearly describes our position and authority in Christ.

After I had spent several minutes taking authority in Christ through prayer and reading Scripture, Harry fell flat on his stomach in front of me. "Lord Jesus, I need You!" he cried out. I led him in a prayer of commitment to Christ. And when Harry finally stood up he was free. He embraced Wayne and me with a childlike joy he had never experienced before.

Even though Harry was set free from Satan's control of his life, he had trouble staying free. He was kind of like an alcoholic who comes to Christ. When an alcoholic receives Christ, he is totally alive spiritually. But unless God intervenes in an unusual way, he has to live with the damage he has done to his liver and with the patterns, habits, and cravings which were ingrained in his brain over the years. Similarly, Harry had been deeply involved in satanic rituals for most of his life. Once he made a decision for Christ, he couldn't just walk away from his past as if it had never happened. He continued to battle the physical, mental, and emotional effects of his bondage.

Other Satanists made several attempts on Harry's life and harassed him mentally day and night. They contacted Harry and agreed to stop their demonic mental assault on him if he would sign an agreement not to share his testimony again as he had at our church. Harry signed the agreement, and I haven't heard from him since. *Never* make a deal with the devil.

A Trap as Old as the Bible

How do people like Harry get trapped in the quicksand of Satan's control in the first place? What are some of the traps the devil has set to keep us from the freedom which is ours in Christ?

One of his major traps is his appeal to the human desire for spiritual knowledge and power. We crave a secret knowledge that is not normally available to the ordinary person. We want to experience a power that is spiritual and supernatural in origin. Satan knows this. That's why most occult groups and activities promise secret or special information or power that many people find hard to resist.

In a sense, the desire for knowledge and power is God-given. But it is intended to be fulfilled by the knowledge and power that comes from *God*. However, Satan is busy trying to pass off his counterfeits for God's knowledge and power as the real thing. If he can get you to accept his versions of knowledge and power, he has an open door into your life.

The lure of satanic knowledge and power is nothing new. God's people have been warned against it from the earliest times. Just before the nation of Israel entered Canaan, the Promised Land, Moses commanded them:

> You must be very careful lest you be corrupted by the horrible customs of the nations now living there. For example, any Israeli who presents his child to be burned to death as a sacrifice to heathen gods, must be killed. No Israeli may practice black magic, or call on the evil spirits for aid, or be a fortune teller, or be a serpent charmer, medium, or wizard, or call forth the spirits of the dead. Anyone doing these things is an object of horror and disgust to the Lord, and it is because the nations do these things that the Lord your God will displace them. You must walk blamelessly before the Lord your God (Deuteronomy 18:9-13 TLB).

This command is just as important for us today as it was for the Israelites. We live in a world that is just like Canaan. Our society thinks it's okay to seek knowledge and power from spiritists (communicating with spirits of the dead), mediums (witches), palm-readers, psychic counselors, and horoscopes. This was clearly brought home to us when we surveyed 1292 Christian high school students. Approximately one-third of them admitted that they had been involved in spiritual practices God clearly says are wrong.

Some kids argue, "But this stuff really works. My horoscope is right on most of the time." The issue isn't whether or not it works, but whether or not it's right. According to God, it's *not* right, and we shouldn't be fooling around with it.

The dark side of Satan's versions of spiritual knowledge and power mentioned by Moses—animal sacrifice, witchcraft, sorcery—are also thriving in our culture, though not as openly. Police departments are trying to tell your parents, "Wake up! Our kids are not just into drugs and illicit sex. They're into *Satanism*. We've seen the blood and the mutilated animals." It's getting so bad that one of the animal control agencies in our area will no longer release a black dog or cat for fear that it will become the victim of satanic abuse.

Every unthinkable act that Moses warned Israel not to get involved in—from horoscopes to animal and human sacrifice—is in place and operating in our culture today. And they all have their root in Satan's deception.

Knowledge from the Dark Side

Many people today are craving extra "hidden" knowledge about life. They don't want to hear what God has to say. They want information and direction from someone who *"knows"*: a psychic, a channeler, a palm-reader, a card-reader, or the spirit of a dead friend or relative.

The Bible is very clear about seeking knowledge and direction from anyone but God: "Do not turn to mediums or spiritists; do not seek them out to be defiled by them.... As for the person who turns to mediums and to spiritists, to play the harlot after them, I will also set My face against that person and will cut him off from among his people. . . . A man or a woman who is a medium or a spiritist shall surely be put to death" (Leviticus 19:31; 20:6,27).

In our country, we're about as far away from obeying that command as we can be. We have people channeling on TV and radio programs, and they're considered celebrities. One newspaper report stated that more women in Los Angeles visit spiritists than professional counselors. You can attend a psychic fair in practically any city in our land and get a personal spiritual "reading." The reader is either a fake or a spiritual medium who enters a trance and seemingly receives instruction for you from the spiritual world. Far from being seen as a black mark on society, these people are often revered as highly as doctors and ministers for their "expertise."

Mediums—Phony and for Real

Where do mediums and spiritists get their "amazing" information and insights? Many of them are being influenced by demons, but much of what is called spiritism or psychic activity is no more than a clever, human trick. These so-called spiritists give what is referred to as "cold readings." You go to them for advice or direction, and they ask you a few simple questions. Based on the answers you give, they make general observations which are probably true of most people in your situation. But you are so impressed with the accuracy of their "revelations" that you start tipping off all kinds of details which then they can work into their "reading." This is not demonic; it's just a mental and verbal magic trick.

The mediums and spiritists that God warned against in Leviticus and Deuteronomy were not con artists but people who possessed and passed on knowledge which didn't come through clever observation. These people have opened themselves up to the spirit world and become channels of knowledge from Satan. The phony with his cold readings is only interested in taking your money. But the false knowledge and direction which comes from Satan through a medium is intended to rob you of your spiritual victory and freedom.

There's big money in these psychic/con artist operations, and a lot of magicians are raking it in. Many people crave to know something extra about their lives and their future, and they will pay well if they think someone can give them the inside information they desire.

The Down Side of Seeking the Dark Side

The Old Testament is full of illustrations of kings, false prophets, and mediums leading the nation of Israel in rebellion against God. One of the more well-known cases was Israel's first king. Saul began well by seeking God's guidance and was appointed by Samuel as king of Israel (1 Samuel 9). And he served well until his rebellion against God's will (1 Samuel 15), a sin which God says is the same as the sin of witchcraft (verse 23).

Why did Saul sin and reject the Word of the Lord? Because he feared the voice of the people more than the voice of God—a problem too many people struggle with in our world today. The problem of rebellion is the worst problem in the world.

Although Saul was sorry that he sinned (or at least sorry that he was caught!), there is no evidence to suggest that he really turned his back on his sinful ways. Like many people who disobey God, he tried to fix his mistake. But it was too late, and "the Spirit of the LORD departed from Saul, and an evil spirit from the LORD terrorized him" (1 Samuel 16:14).

This is a tough passage for two reasons. First, it seems to be saying that a person can lose the Holy Spirit by an act of disobedience. But we need to understand that the Holy Spirit in the Old Testament only came upon certain people at certain times for certain tasks. This unique equipping is not the same as the personal relationship in the Spirit that we enjoy with God as His children today.

Beginning after the cross, the church is identified by the indwelling presence of the Holy Spirit (Ephesians 1:13,14). Jesus promised that no one will snatch us out of His hand (John 10:28), and Paul assured that nothing—not even disobedience—can separate us from the love of God (Romans 8:35-39). We are secure in Christ and His Spirit dwells in us through faith in the work of Christ on the cross. The Holy Spirit doesn't come and go in response to our obedience or disobedience.

The second problem concerns the troubling idea that an evil spirit could come from the Lord. But we must remember that God is supreme, and He can use Satan and his demons as a means to discipline His people as He did with Saul. This is no different from God using a godless nation like Assyria as "the rod of

My anger" to discipline His people (Isaiah 10:5,6). God is God, and He can use demons to accomplish His will if He wants to.

Even the church is allowed to turn an immoral member over to Satan "to punish him, in the hope that his soul will be saved when our Lord Jesus Christ returns" (1 Corinthians 5:5 TLB). Why? So the world and its ruler, the devil, can do a number on such a person in order to bring about a real change.

Whenever the evil spirit came upon Saul, David would play his harp and the evil spirit would depart (1 Samuel 16:23). How dense we are when it comes to understanding the biblical importance of music in the spiritual realm! During the reign of David, over 4000 musicians were assigned to sing in the temple night and day (1 Chronicles 9:33; 23:5). It is the mark of Spirit-filled Christians to sing and make melody in their hearts to the Lord and speak to each other in psalms, hymns, and spiritual songs (Ephesians 5:18-20).

On the other side of the truth we find the destructive power of some secular music. Harry, the satanic high priest, showed me (Neil) numerous symbols on popular record albums indicating links to Satanism. He told me that about 85 percent of today's heavy metal and punk music groups are "owned" by Satanists. They have unwittingly sold themselves to Satanism in exchange for fame and fortune. Few of these artists actually practice Satanism, but most are hopelessly lost and lead others astray through the godless message in their music.

After Samuel the prophet died, Saul's twisted thirst for spiritual knowledge led him to seek guidance from a medium—the witch of Endor. Coming to the witch in disguise, Saul persuaded her to call up the spirit of dead Samuel (1 Samuel 28:8-19). But the scheme backfired when God permitted Samuel himself to return, terrifying the witch. Samuel's message to Saul was nothing but bad news. He said that the Philistines would defeat Israel and that Saul and his sons would be killed (verse 19). It happened just as Samuel said.

God clearly forbids communicating with the dead (Isaiah 8:19,20), and the story of the rich man and Lazarus teaches the present-day impossibility of communicating with the dead (Luke 16:19-31). When a psychic claims to have contacted the dead, don't believe it. When a psychologist claims to have taken a client back to a former life through hypnosis, don't believe it. When a New Age medium reports to have channeled a person from the past into the present, realize that it is nothing more than a demon or the trick of a con artist.

An Old Idea in New Clothing

The thirst for knowledge and power has lured many youth to seek guidance from mediums and spiritists, and from such occultic practices as fortune-telling, tarot cards, palm-reading, Ouija boards, astrology, magic charming, and automatic writing. "Is it because there is no God in Israel that you are going to inquire of Baal-zebub [Satan]?" Elijah lamented (2 Kings 1:3). Young people all around us are ignoring the God who promises to love them and guide them, and are instead seeking light and peace in the kingdom of darkness.

Don't be carried away by the prospect of knowledge and power which is luring so many youth in our culture away from God. Those who seek knowledge and power from the dark side will greatly interfere with the work of God, deceiving many by the counterfeit forces they employ. Other people will thirst after power to such an extent that they will even sacrifice their own children to demons (Psalm 106:36-38). We can verify firsthand from our counseling experience that these kinds of things are actually happening today.

Let these sad words from the Bible remind us that even believers can be lured away from the knowledge and power of God by our enemy. And let them encourage us to seek knowledge and power from God alone:

> But Israel was soon overfed; yes, fat and bloated; then, in plenty, they forsook their God. They shrugged away the Rock of their salvation. Israel began to follow foreign gods, and Jehovah was very angry; he was jealous of his people. They sacrificed to heathen gods, to new gods never before worshiped. They spurned the Rock who had made them, forgetting it was God who had given them birth (Deuteronomy 32:15-18 TLB).

Truth Encounter

Read: Deuteronomy 18:9-13; 1 Samuel 15:23

Reflect: 1. Why should we be careful not to get involved with mediums or spiritists? What are some of the possible side effects that might follow if someone was to open himself up to this kind of cultic activity?

2. Why is rebellion like the sin of divination or witchcraft? How does rebellion relate to arrogance?

3. How was music used in the worship of God in Old Testament times? Why must we carefully select the music we listen to?

4. What kind of New Age teaching or practices do you see in your school? On television? In your community? How can you avoid being drawn into New Age thinking in our world today?

Respond: One of the big dangers we face is our curiosity about the New Age and occult practices. The lure of satanic knowledge and power is something God warns us to watch out for. Pray and ask God to help you cut off your craving for hidden knowledge or power. Ask God to reveal to your mind the practices you have been involved in, so that you can confess and renounce them.

8

Enticed to Do It Your Way

I (Dave) remember one of my earliest experiences with temptation. One day as a young boy, two of my friends and I jumped on our bikes for a trip down to the local department store. It was a long ride, so we had time to talk. At first we discussed what we wanted to buy: packages of exploding caps made for cap guns. But as we neared the store, the conversation took a bad turn. We began to discuss how easy it would be to steal the caps. The idea of getting something for nothing was tempting, and we decided to do it.

We entered the store and went straight to the toy section. I was both excited and scared about the heist as each of my friends slipped a package of caps inside his pocket. Suddenly it was my turn, and they stepped aside to give me a clear view of the prize.

My heart was pounding so hard I thought it was going to explode out of my chest. I knew it was wrong, but I didn't want to be labeled a chicken. So I reached for the caps...then stopped. I remembered the hidden cameras. I glanced up at the huge, shiny bubble on the ceiling made of one-way glass. There was a camera inside that bubble. My brother-in-law worked at the store and had told me all about the camera system. It would be crazy to try to steal something; we were being watched!

I sheepishly announced to my friends that I wasn't going to do it. They grumbled at me and called me a chicken, then we headed for the exit. Two men from store security suddenly blocked our escape. "Where are the caps, boys?" they asked, glaring at us.

"What caps?" my two friends replied in unison, faking their innocence.

"Come on, boys, we saw you take them," the security men fired back.

My two friends fell apart and cried like babies. I tried to hide my relief that I had chickened out at the last minute. It was one time in my life when, thanks to the grace of God and a security camera, I didn't yield to temptation.

In this chapter we want to talk about temptation so you can easily recognize it and quickly refuse Satan's invitation to do things your own way.

What Is Temptation?

Temptation means being enticed to have genuine needs met through the world, the flesh, and the devil instead of through Christ (Philippians 4:19). Every temptation is an invitation to do things our own way instead of God's way.

Most of us won't often be tempted to commit obvious sins like armed robbery, murder, or rape. Satan is too clever and sneaky for that. He knows that we will recognize obvious wrong and refuse to act on it. Instead, he likes to entice us to push something good beyond the boundary of the will of God until it becomes sin.

Paul wrote, "I can do anything I want to if Christ has not said no, but some of these things aren't good for me. Even if I am allowed to do them, I'll refuse to if I think they might get such a grip on me that I can't easily stop when I want to" (1 Corinthians 6:12 TLB). Paul saw nothing but green lights in every direction of the Christian life. Everything is good and lawful for us because we are free from sin and no longer under the condemnation of the law. But Paul also knew that if we go 80 MPH in any of these good and lawful directions we will eventually run the red light of God's will, and that's sin.

The following statements show the sinful results in a number of areas where we are tempted to take the good things that God created beyond the boundary of God's will:

- physical rest becomes laziness
- quietness becomes an unwillingness to talk to anyone
- ability to make money becomes greed
- enjoyment of life becomes too much partying, drinking, etc.
- physical pleasure becomes lust
- interest in the possessions of others becomes coveting
- enjoyment of food becomes gluttony

- taking good care of yourself becomes selfishness
- talking with others becomes gossip
- anger becomes rage and bad temper
- judgment becomes criticism
- same-sex friendship becomes homosexuality
- opposite-sex friendship becomes immorality
- generosity becomes wastefulness
- carefulness and caution become fear

Some Christians confuse temptation with sin. Temptation is not the same as sin. Even Jesus was "tempted in all things as we are." But finish the verse: "Yet without sin" (Hebrews 4:15). As long as we are in the world we are exposed to temptation just like Jesus was. But He didn't sin, and we don't have to sin either (1 Corinthians 10:13). Temptation is like seeing Satan's face through the window; sin is like unlocking and opening the door, making it possible for him to come in. Remember, God's boundaries are not restrictive; they are protective.

Channels of Temptation

You will be better prepared to resist temptation in your life when you realize that, according to the Scriptures, there are only three channels through which Satan will entice you to act outside of God's will. They are talked about in 1 John 2:15-17: "Do not love the world, nor the things in the world. If anyone loves the world, the love of the Father is not in him. For all that is in the world, the lust of the flesh and the lust of the eyes and the boastful pride of life, is not from the Father, but is from the world. And the world is passing away, and also its lusts; but the one who does the will of God abides forever."

The three channels of temptation are the *lust of the flesh*, the *lust of the eyes*, and the *pride of life*. The lust of the flesh tempts us to fulfill our physical appetites (food, sex, comfort, etc.) in a sinful, worldly way. The lust of the eyes tempts us to do what we think is best instead of obeying the Bible. The pride of life tempts us to get all the attention and glory for ourselves.

Satan tempted both Adam and Jesus through each of these three channels. Adam failed in a big way, and we still suffer the results of his failure and fall. But Jesus Christ met Satan's three-level temptation head-on and succeeded triumphantly. In Him we have the example and the power to conquer every temptation Satan throws at us.

The Lust of the Flesh

Satan first approached Eve through the channel of the lust of the flesh. He planted a doubt in her mind about the fruit of the tree when he said: "Has God said, 'You shall not eat from any tree of the garden'?" (Genesis 3:1). Actually, God didn't say, "any tree," only the one tree. Satan distorts the word of God. Eve answered, "God has said, 'You shall not eat from it or touch it'" (verse 3). Eve also distorted God's word when she added, "or touch it." But Satan had aroused her appetite for the forbidden fruit, and she "saw that the tree was good for food" (verse 6) and ate some of it. Yielding to the lust of the flesh contributed to Adam and Eve's downfall.

Satan also challenged Jesus through the channel of the lust of the flesh. Our Lord had been fasting (going without food) for 40 days when Satan tempted Him at the weakness of his hunger: "If You are the Son of God, command that these stones become bread" (Matthew 4:3).

Satan doesn't know everything, but he's not blind either. He learned that Jesus was hungry by watching Him go without food for 40 days. He's watching us too, looking for soft spots and weakness in our physical appetites for food, rest, comfort, and sex. Temptation is greatest when we are especially hungry, tired, or lonely.

The temptation of the lust of the flesh is designed to draw us away from the will of God to please ourselves (Galatians 5:16,17). There is nothing sinful about eating. Eating is a physical need, and God created food so we could meet that need. But about one fruit in the garden God said to Adam and Eve, "Don't eat it." By eating, Adam and Eve went against God's will.

In the same way, there was nothing wrong with Jesus eating bread at the end of His fast, except that it wasn't the Father's will for Him to do so yet. Jesus replied: "Man shall not live on bread alone, but on every word that proceeds out of the mouth of God" (Matthew 4:4). No matter how desirable a loaf of bread seemed to Jesus in His hunger, He was not about to act outside of the Father's will by accepting Satan's offer. The life that Jesus modeled was a life totally dependent on God the Father (John 5:30; 6:57; 8:42; 14:10; 17:7). All temptation is an attempt by Satan to get us to live our lives independently of God.

When Satan tempts us through the channel of the lust of the flesh, he will invite us to meet our physical needs in ways that are outside the boundary of God's will. Eating is necessary and right, but eating too much, eating the wrong kinds of foods, and allowing food to rule our lives are wrong. God intended sex to be beautiful and good. But sex outside of marriage, homosexuality, and selfish sex are out-of-bounds and lead to bondage.

Whenever you feel enticed to meet a physical need by acting outside of God's will, you are being tempted through the lust of the flesh. When you resist the temptations of the lust of the flesh, you are declaring your dependence on God for your natural needs.

The Lust of the Eyes

The second channel of temptation Satan used on Adam and Eve was based on a lie. Satan lied about what would happen if Adam and Eve disobeyed God. God had said that disobedience would lead to death, but Satan said, "You surely shall not die!" (Genesis 3:4). "Don't listen to God. Do what *you* think is right," he urged Eve. The forbidden fruit was a delight to her eyes (verse 6), so she and Adam ignored God's command and did what they decided was best for them.

The lust of the eyes gradually draws us away from the Word of God and eats away at our confidence in God. We see what the world has to offer and desire those things more than our relationship with God. We begin to trust in our own view of life more than in God's commands and promises. We get excited about all the stuff we see around us and grab for all we can get. We convince ourselves that we need it and that God wants us to have it.

Instead of trusting God wholeheartedly, we adopt a "prove it to me" attitude. That's what Satan's second temptation of Jesus was all about: "If You are the Son of God, throw Yourself down [from the top of the temple]; for it is written, 'He will give His angels charge concerning You'; and 'On their hands they will bear You up, lest You strike Your foot against a stone'" (Matthew 4:6).

But Jesus wasn't about to play Satan's "show me" game. He replied, "It is written, 'You shall not put the LORD your God to the test'" (verse 7).

When you resist the temptations of the lust of the eyes, you are choosing to follow the Word of God instead of your own idea of how to run your life. The righteous shall live by faith in the written Word of God and not demand that God prove Himself by fulfilling our wishes, no matter how noble they are.

The Pride of Life

The third channel of temptation is at the heart of the New Age movement: the temptation to direct our own future, to rule our own world, to be our own god. Satan tempted Eve with the forbidden fruit: "The day you eat from it your eyes will be opened, and you will be like God, knowing good and evil" (Genesis 3:5). Satan's offer was an appeal to the ability God gave us to rule. "Don't be satisfied ruling *under* God," he seemed to say, "when you have the potential to be God." When Eve was convinced that "the tree was desirable to make one wise" (verse 6), she and Adam ate.

Satan's promise that the couple would become like God was nothing more than a lie. When Adam and Eve yielded to his temptation, they didn't become the gods of this world as he claimed they would. Instead, they fell from their position of rulership with God, and Satan became the god of this world—exactly as he had planned.

Satan tried the same trick on Jesus: "The devil took Him to a very high mountain, and showed Him all the kingdoms of the world and their glory; and he said to Him, 'All these things will I give You, if You fall down and worship me'" (Matthew 4:8,9). Satan was the god of this world because Adam and Eve gave up that role at the first temptation. So the kingdoms of the world were his to offer to Jesus.

When you think about it, however, Satan's offer was pretty ridiculous. Why would Jesus be tempted to worship Satan in exchange for the world when He already owned the universe? So He replied, "Begone, Satan! For it is written, 'You shall worship the LORD your God, and serve Him only'" (verse 10).

The temptation of the pride of life is intended to steer us away from the worship of God and destroy our obedience to God by urging us to take charge of our own lives. Whenever you feel that you don't need God's help or direction, that you can handle your life without going to Him, that you don't need to submit to anyone, beware: That's the pride of life.

You may think you are serving yourself, but whenever you stop worshiping and serving God you are really worshiping and serving Satan—which is what he wants more than anything else. Instead, your life should be marked by worshipful humility and obedience to God (1 Peter 5:5-11; John 15:8-10).

Remember, there are three critical issues reflected in these channels of temptation: 1) the will of God in your life, seen through your dependence on God; 2) the Word of God in your life, seen through your confidence in God; and 3) the worship of God in your life, seen through your obedience to God. Every temptation that Satan throws at you will challenge one or more of these values. He will watch you to learn where you are weak and will tempt you in any area that you leave unguarded.

Why do we entertain tempting thoughts that are contrary to God's Word and God's will? Let's face it— we want to. We're not tempted to overeat foods we don't like, to think impure thoughts about unattractive guys or girls, or to shoplift something we don't want. The devil's hook is his guarantee that what we think we want and need outside God's will can satisfy us. Don't believe it. You can never satisfy the desires of the flesh. Instead, "Blessed are those who hunger and thirst for righteousness, for they shall be satisfied" (Matthew 5:6). Only right relationships, living by the power of the Holy Spirit, and experiencing the fruit of the Spirit will satisfy you.

The Way of Escape

First Corinthians 10:13 is the shining good news in the midst of our fears and concerns about temptation: "No temptation has overtaken you but such as is common to man; and God is faithful, who will not allow you to be tempted beyond what you are able, but with the temptation will provide the way of escape also, that you may be able to endure it."

Where is the escape hatch that Paul is talking about here? In the same place temptation starts: in our mind. Every temptation is first a thought introduced to our mind by our own evil desires or the devil himself. If you hold that thought and consider acting it out, you will eventually do it, and that's sin. Instead Paul tells us to take every thought captive to the obedience of Christ (2 Corinthians 10:5). The first step for escaping temptation is to capture every thought as soon as it steps through the doorway of your mind.

Once you have halted an incoming thought, the next step is to check it out to see if it passes the eight-part test based on Philippians 4:8 for what we should think about:

1. Does this thought line up with God's truth?
2. Does it suggest that I do something honorable?
3. Is it right?
4. Is it pure?
5. Will the outcome of this thought be lovely?
6. Will the result be something to admire?
7. Will it contribute to excellence in my life?
8. Is it something for which I can praise God?

If the answer to any of these questions is no, kick the thought out immediately. Don't have anything more to do with it. If it keeps coming back, keep saying no. When you learn to respond to tempting thoughts by stopping them at the door of your mind, evaluating them on the basis of God's Word, and dismissing those which fail the test, you have found the way of escape that God's Word promises.

On the other hand, if a thought comes into your mind and it passes the Philippians 4:8 test of truth, honor, righteousness, etc., "let your mind dwell on these things" (verse 8) and "practice these things" (verse 9). "And the God of peace shall be with you" (verse 9), which is a much better result than the pain and stress which follows when we yield to tempting thoughts and become involved in sinful behavior.

Confess and Resist

"But sometimes I yield to temptation and sin," some Christians complain. "I confess my sin, but when I'm tempted again, I sin again. It seems like I'm riding a roller coaster of ups and downs—sin, confess, sin, confess, sin, confess—and I can't get off."

People who are caught in the sin-confess cycle eventually begin to lose hope that they can experience any real victory over sin. Sheer willpower can't keep them from repeating the sin they just confessed, and Satan pours on the guilt.

Sin which is allowed to reign is like a dog that gets into your yard, bites you on the leg, and won't let go. First you're tempted from the other side of the fence: "Come on. Everyone else does it. Open the gate— you'll get away with it." But when you give in to the temptation, the tune changes: "You opened the gate! You opened the gate!" The tempter changes roles and becomes the accuser. You beat on yourself for your failure and cry out to God for forgiveness. He forgives you, but the dog is still there.

Why not cry out to God and beat on the dog instead of yourself? James 4:7 tells us, "Submit therefore to God. Resist the devil and he will flee from you." We must confess our sin, but there is another important step which breaks the cycle: sin-confess-*resist*. We must resist Satan and command him aloud to leave if we are going to experience victory over sin.

The apostle John wrote: "My little children, I am writing these things to you that you may not sin. And if anyone sins, we have an Advocate [defender] with the Father, Jesus Christ the righteous" (1 John 2:1). We must turn to our righteous defender and resist our adversary if we are to experience victory and freedom over temptation and sin.

Truth Encounter

Read: 1 Corinthians 10:13; James 4:7; 2 Corinthians 10:5; Philippians 4:8

Reflect: 1. What are some common ways that Satan and his demons try to tempt us in the area of our physical appetites?

2. What are some common ways that we are tempted to trust in ourselves and our own knowledge rather than God and His Word?

3. What does it mean to take every thought captive?

4. What does Philippians 4:8 ask us to think through in relation to taking thoughts captive? Can you name some of the eight steps talked about in the verse?

Respond: Read Philippians 4:8 once again. Now think of an issue you're struggling with in your life and imagine the possible choices you have. Pray and ask God to reveal to you if your choices line up with His Word. Are they honorable, right, and pure? Will they please God?

9

Don't Believe Everything You Hear

When I (Dave) was in junior high I was a wrestler. I remember the tournament in which I competed for the championship. I had wrestled all day and won every match. Now I would face my toughest opponent. He would have to be a good wrestler to make it to the final round. But I was pumped. I felt like I could beat anybody.

When I saw the boy I was going to wrestle for the championship, my heart sank. It was my coach's son. The coach stood silently at the edge of the mat. But I knew he wanted his son to win. What father wouldn't? It was like I was going for the championship without a coach. My mind filled with doubts. I began to question my abilities. Phrases like, "I'm not good enough" and "I can't beat him," rattled through my mind. I soon convinced myself that there was no way I could ever beat the coach's son.

Well, I lost. But I can't say that my opponent's wrestling skills defeated me that day. I lost the match before I even stepped onto the mat by believing the accusations in my brain.

Teenagers seem to have one sad thing in common: All kids are pretty good at putting themselves down like I did that day. They say, "I'm not important, I'm not qualified, I'm no good." It's amazing how many young Christians are paralyzed in their witness and growth because they think and feel they are worthless.

This discouraging inner criticism may have its roots in the kingdom of darkness. Next to temptation, perhaps the most frequent and insistent attack Satan throws at us is accusation. In Christ we *are* important, we *are* qualified, we *are* good. Satan can do nothing to change our position in Christ and our worth to God. But he can defeat us if he can trick us into believing his lies that we are of little value to God or other people.

Satan's two favorite moves are temptation and accusation. He uses them to pin us down and defeat us. He comes along and says, "Why don't you try it? Everybody does it. Besides, you can get away with it. Who's going to know?" Then as soon as we fall for his tempting line, he changes his tune to accusation: "What kind of a Christian are you to do such a thing? You're a sad excuse for a child of God. You'll never get away with it. You might as well give up because God has already given up on you."

Satan is called "the accuser of the brethren... who accuses them before our God day and night" (Revelation 12:10). We have all heard his lying, hateful voice in our hearts and minds. He never seems to let up on us. Many Christians are always discouraged and defeated because they believe his lies about them. And those who give in to his accusations end up being robbed of the freedom that God intends His people to enjoy. One defeated Christian wrote:

> My old feelings that life isn't worth the trouble keep coming back. I'm scared, lonely, confused, and very desperate. I know deep down that God can overcome this, but I can't get past this block. I can't even pray. When I try, things get in my way. When I'm feeling good and I begin putting into action what I know God wants me to do, I'm stopped dead in my tracks by those voices and a force so strong I can't continue. I'm so close to giving in to those voices that I almost can't fight them anymore. I just want some peace.

Putting the Accuser
in His Place

The good news is that we don't have to listen to Satan's accusations and live in defeat. Zechariah 3:1-10 contains an important truth we need to grab hold of in order to stand by faith against Satan's accusations and to live righteously in the service of God.

The Lord showed the prophet Zechariah a heavenly scene in which Satan's accusations of God's people are put into proper perspective: "Then he showed me Joshua the high priest standing before the angel of the LORD, and Satan standing at his right hand to accuse him. And the LORD said to Satan, 'The LORD rebuke you, Satan! Indeed, the LORD who has chosen Jerusalem rebuke you! Is this not a brand plucked from the fire?' Now Joshua was clothed with filthy garments and standing before the angel" (verses 1-3).

The Lord Rebukes Satan

Look at the cast of characters in this scene. It looks like a heavenly courtroom. The judge is God the Father. The prosecuting attorney is Satan. The defense attorney is Jesus. And the accused defendant is Joshua the high priest, who represents all of God's people, including you and me.

In Hebrew history, when the high priest entered God's presence in the holy of holies (the place where the sacrifice for sin was offered) each year, it was a very serious occasion. The priest had to perform special ceremonies to make sure he was clean before God. If the priest wasn't just right before God, he could be struck dead on the spot. The priest wore bells on the hem of his robe so those outside the holy of holies could tell if he was still alive and moving. They even tied a rope around his ankle so he could be dragged out if he dropped dead in God's presence.

So here is a high priest named Joshua standing in God's presence with filthy garments representing the sins of Israel. Bad news! Satan the accuser says, "Look at him, God. He's filthy. He deserves to be struck dead." But God rebukes the accuser and puts him in his place. "You're not the judge, and you cannot pass sentence on My people," God seems to say in His rebuke. "I have rescued Joshua from the flames of judgment, and your accusations are false."

This courtroom scene is going on night and day for every child of God. Satan keeps pointing out our faults and weaknesses to God and demands that He zap us for being less than perfect. But our defense attorney in heaven is Jesus Christ, and He has never lost a case before God the judge. Satan can't make his accusations stick because Jesus Christ took our sins at the cross. He has made us right with God and stands before God in our defense (Romans 8:33,34).

While Satan accuses us before God, he and his demons also accuse us by bombarding our minds with false thoughts of how unworthy and unrighteous we are in God's sight: "How could you do that and be a Christian? You're not really a child of God." But Satan is not our judge; he is only our *accuser*. Yet if we listen to him and believe him, we will begin to live out these accusations as if they were a sentence we must serve.

When Satan's accusations of unworthiness attack you, don't pay attention to them. Instead respond, "Satan, I have put my trust in Christ, and I am a child of God in Him. Like Joshua the high priest, I have been rescued by God from the fire of judgment. He has declared me righteous. You're not the judge. All you can do is accuse me—and I don't buy it."

The Lord Removes Our Filthy Garments

The reason Satan's accusations are false is because God has solved the problem of our filthy garments, meaning our sin. Zechariah's description of the heavenly courtroom scene continues: "And he spoke and said to those who were standing before him saying, 'Remove the filthy garments from him.' Again he said to him, 'See, I have taken your iniquity away from you and will clothe you with festal robes.' Then I said, 'Let them put a clean turban on his head.' So they put a clean turban on his head and clothed him with garments, while the angel of the LORD was standing by" (3:4,5).

God has not only declared us righteous, but He has removed our filthy garments of sin and clothed us with His righteousness. Notice that the change of wardrobe is something that *God* does, not us. In ourselves, we don't have any garments of righteousness to put on that will satisfy God. He changes us when we give our lives to Him in faith.

The Lord Asks Us to Respond

Having rebuked Satan and provided our righteousness, the Lord calls us to respond with obedience: "If you will walk in My ways, and if you will perform My service, then you will also govern My house and also have charge of My courts, and I will grant you free access among these who are standing here" (Zechariah 3:7).

In calling us to walk in His ways and perform His service, the Lord is simply calling us to live out our identity in Christ through our obedience. This means living by faith instead of fear. It means crucifying the flesh on a daily basis and walking according to the Spirit. It means believing that we are dead to sin and alive to God and not allowing sin to rule in our bodies. It means taking every thought captive to the obedience of Christ and being transformed by the renewing of our minds.

If we walk in obedience, God promises that we will govern His house and have charge of His courts. This means that we will share in His authority in the spiritual world, able to live victoriously over Satan and sin. He also promises us an open line of communication with the Father. As we operate in His authority and live in fellowship and harmony with Him, our daily victory and fruitfulness are assured.

What's the Difference?

You may be thinking, "When the devil throws his accusations at me, I feel bummed out. But sometimes the Holy Spirit's conviction bums me out too. How can I tell the difference between Satan's accusations and the Spirit's conviction?"

Paul shows us the difference between the two in 2 Corinthians 7:9,10:

> I now rejoice, not that you were made sorrowful, but that you were made sorrowful to the point of repentance; for you were made sorrowful according to the will of God, in order that you might not suffer loss in anything through us. For the sorrow that is according to the will of God produces a repentance without regret, leading to salvation; but the sorrow of the world produces death.

The devil's accusations and the Holy Spirit's conviction both bring feelings of sorrow. But the sorrow from Satan's accusations leads to death. In other words, the devil wants us to feel bad in order to destroy us. He wants us to give up and quit following Christ.

In contrast, the sorrow of conviction is allowed by God to prompt us to repent, which leads to life. God isn't beating us into the ground with sorrow. He wants our feelings of sorrow over our sin to bring us to Him so we can experience forgiveness and freedom.

Every young Christian is faced with the choice of walking by the Spirit or by the flesh on a daily basis. When we choose to walk according to the flesh, the Holy Spirit brings conviction because we are not acting in harmony with who we really are. If we continue in the flesh we will feel the sorrow of conviction.

"How do I know which kind of sorrow I'm experiencing?" you may ask. "They feel the same." Figure out whether your feelings reflect the truth or a lie, and you will identify their source. Do you feel guilty, worthless, or stupid? That's a sorrow caused by accusation, because those feelings don't reflect truth. You are no longer guilty; you have been forgiven through your faith in Christ. You are not worthless; Jesus gave His life for you. You are not stupid; you can do all things through Christ.

When you find lies lurking beneath your feelings of sorrow—especially if your feelings keep pounding you into the ground—you are being falsely accused. Even if you changed you wouldn't feel any better, because Satan would then find something else to bug you about. To get rid of the sorrow of accusation you must submit yourself to God and resist the devil and his lies.

But if you feel bummed out because you're not living the way God wants you to live, it's the Holy Spirit calling you to admit on the basis of 1 John 1:9, "Dear Lord, I was wrong." As soon as you confess and repent, God says, "I'm glad you shared that with Me.

You're cleansed; now get on with life." And you walk away free. The sorrow is gone, and you have a new determination to obey God in the area of your failure.

The difference between accusation and conviction is clearly seen in the lives of two of Jesus' disciples: Judas and Peter. Somehow Judas allowed Satan to deceive him into betraying Jesus for 30 pieces of silver (Luke 22:3-5). When Judas realized what he had done, he hanged himself. Was his suicide the result of Satan's accusation or of God's conviction? It had to be accusation because it drove Judas to kill himself. Accusation leads to death; conviction leads to repentance and life.

Peter also failed Jesus by denying Him (Luke 22:33,34). The sorrow Peter felt was every bit as painful as that which Judas experienced. But Peter's sorrow was from conviction which eventually led him to repent (John 21:15-17).

When your feelings of sorrow pound you into the ground and drive you from God, you are being accused by Satan. Resist it. But when your sorrow draws you to Christ to confess your wrong, you are being convicted by the Spirit. Yield to it and repent.

According to Revelation 12:10, Satan's continuing work is to accuse God's children. But Christ's continuing work is to pray for us (Hebrews 7:25). We have a persistent enemy, but we have an even more persistent, eternal Savior who defends us before the Father on the basis of our faith in Him (1 John 2:1).

The Quicksand of Accusation

It is very important to our daily victory in Christ that we learn to resist the accusations of Satan. We have all felt like worthless nobodies at times. When we feel like worthless nobodies we act like worthless nobodies, and our lives suffer until we resist Satan and return to a life of victory.

But Satan never gives up. He will try to get us down more often and keep us down longer by firing at us one false accusation after another. If we fail to keep resisting him we may become targets for even more serious attacks from Satan.

Janelle's story is an extreme case, but it shows what can happen to a Christian who fails to take a stand against Satan the accuser.

Janelle was a young Christian with severe emotional problems who was brought to me (Neil) by her elderly pastor. Janelle's fiancé, Curt, came with them. After introducing me to Janelle and Curt, the pastor started to leave. "Wait a minute," I said. "I'd prefer that you stay with us."

"I've got a bad heart," the pastor replied.

"I don't think anything will happen here today that will affect your heart," I assured. (I had no idea what was about to happen!) "Besides, you're her pastor, and I would appreciate your prayer support." The pastor reluctantly agreed.

As Janelle told me her story I realized that Satan the accuser had really done a number on her. She had been the victim of one abuse after another as a child and teenager. Her background also included a sick relationship with a previous boyfriend who was involved in the occult. Over the years she had come to believe Satan's lies that she was the cause of her troubles and that she was of no value to God or anybody else. Her view of herself was down in the mud.

Recognizing Satan's familiar strategy, I said, "Janelle, we can help you with your problems because there is a battle going on for your mind which God has given us authority to win." As soon as I spoke those words Janelle suddenly went blank. She sat as still as a stone, eyes glazed over and staring into space.

"Have you ever seen her behave like this?" I asked her pastor and fiancé.

"No," they answered, wide-eyed. They were really frightened.

"Well, there's nothing to worry about. I've seen it before," I said. "We're going to take authority over it, but it's important that you two make sure your relationship with God is right to keep the demonic influence from transferring to you."

I led the pastor in a prayer similar to those found in Chapter 12 of this book. When I turned to lead Curt in prayer, he started to shake. "Curt, is there something between you and God that's not right? If so, I suggest you get it cleared up right now." Under the circumstances, Curt didn't need much prompting! He began confessing sin in his life, including the fact that he and Janelle had been sleeping together. I counseled Curt to end that practice, and he said he would. All the while Janelle sat motionless, totally blanked out.

After we had prayed together about getting his life straight with God, I gave Curt a sheet of paper with a prayer on it to read. As soon as Curt began reading the prayer, Janelle snapped to life. She let out a growl, then lashed out and slapped the paper out of Curt's hands. Satan tried to use the suddenness of her actions to frighten us, and for an instant I was startled. But it was just another of his tactics designed to make us shrink back in fear. I addressed the demonic influence in Janelle: "In the name of Christ and by His authority, I bind you to that chair and I command you to sit there."

I wish I could have videotaped Janelle that day in order to show skeptics what happens when Satan is confronted by God's authority. It was as if Wonder Woman had tied Janelle to the chair. She just sat there squirming, bound by the ropes of God's authority. Her eyes blazed at Curt with hatred, which was further evidence of the demonic power which was controlling her. Janelle didn't hate Curt; she loved him. They were going to be married. But Satan hated the fact that his strongholds in Curt and Janelle were being torn down, and his hatred was displayed on Janelle's face.

Curt finished reading the prayer while Janelle continued to squirm in her chair. Then I prayed, "Lord, we declare our dependence on You, for apart from Christ we can do nothing. Now, in the name and authority of the Lord Jesus Christ, we command Satan and all his forces to release Janelle and to remain bound so she will be free to obey God her heavenly Father."

Suddenly Janelle slumped in her chair and snapped out of her trance.

"Do you remember anything we've been doing here?" I asked her.

"No, what happened?" she responded with a puzzled look.

"It's nothing to worry about," I told her. "Somehow Satan has gained a foothold in your life. But we would like to walk you through the steps to freedom in Christ." About an hour later Janelle was free.

What right did Satan have to control Janelle as he did? Only the right she gave him by yielding to his lies. Satan had convinced her that she was practically worthless. So she lived on the fringe of immorality and dabbled in the occult, which gave Satan even more room to work in her life and partially control her. But once Janelle renounced her involvement with sin and Satan, his hold on her was canceled, and he had to leave.

For most of us, Satan's deceptive accusations will not result in the kind of bondage seen in Janelle's life. But if he can cause you to doubt your worth to God or your effectiveness as God's child through his accusations, he can stop you from living for God. Put your feelings to the test. Take every thought captive. Don't believe anything Satan says about you; it's a lie. Believe everything God says about you; it's the truth which will set you free.

Truth Encounter

Read: Zechariah 3:1-7

Reflect: 1. What is an accusation? Does God ever condemn or accuse us? What is the difference between accusation and conviction?

2. What are some of the accusations Satan uses to tear down believers today? Why is it sometimes hard to ignore those accusations?

3. Why do we sometimes try to earn God's love and acceptance even though we already have it? Why is it hard to think of ourselves as righteous even though God says we are?

4. When you feel you are being accused by the enemy, how should you respond? In what ways do you need to act differently when it comes to handling accusation?

Respond: Pray and proclaim to God who you are in Christ. Thank Him that there is now no punishment for those who are in Christ and that Satan isn't able to bring any charges against us that the blood of Christ won't cover.

10

Appearances Can Be Deceiving

Alyce was one of the most pathetic-looking young women I (Neil) have ever met. She was so skinny that she had no more body fat to lose. Her sad, empty eyes told me that she had lost all hope for her life.

Alyce's father said that she was addicted to prescription painkillers. She was a very talented girl and a committed Christian in many ways, but she was also a Darvon junkie who had even been arrested once for illegal possession of prescription drugs. As her father told me her sad story, Alyce sat nodding to herself as if to say, "Yes, that's me, and life is the pits."

Finally I turned to Alyce, took her by the hands, and said, "I want you to tell me who you think you are."

"I'm just a no-good failure," she whimpered.

"You're not a failure," I responded. "You're a child of God." She continued to pour out the negative self-talk, which indicated to me that she had been living under demonic deception. I continued to remind her of the good news of her identity in Christ. The more we talked the more aware I became of Christ's presence ministering to Alyce.

Finally she said, "Do you mean to tell me that all these negative thoughts about myself are nothing but Satan's lies?"

"That's right, Alyce," I nodded. "And as you begin to learn the truth about your identity in Christ, you will be free from the bondage of Satan's lies."

Two weeks later Alyce was enrolled in an intensive 12-week spiritual growth course. At the end of the course she began to take control of her life instead of remaining the victim of Satan's deception. She gained about 25 pounds. And today she's free.

The main theme of the New Testament is the position we enjoy in Christ through our faith in Him. That's the good news: Christ in you and you in Christ. If there is a negative theme in the New Testament which sums up the opposition we face in Satan, it would be deception.

There are at least three ways Satan will try to steer you away from God's truth and deceive you into believing his lies: self-deception, false prophets and teachers, and deceiving spirits. We are the targets for Satan's deception in these areas if we fail to fill our minds with the truth of God's Word.

Beware of Self-Deception

Is it really possible for Christians to deceive themselves? Yes, it is very possible. The Bible tells us about several ways that we as Christians deceive ourselves.

We deceive ourselves when we hear the Word but don't do it (James 1:22; 1 Peter 1:13). We hear the pastor's sermon or the youth leader's Bible study lesson and say, "Wow! What a great truth!" Then we hurry off to share it with someone else without thinking how it applies to our own lives. James said people who hear the Word but don't do what it says deceive themselves (1:22).

We deceive ourselves when we say we have no sin (1 John 1:8). The Bible doesn't say that we *are* sin; it says that it is possible for us to sin and for sin to reside in our bodies (Romans 6:12). We are not sinless saints; we are saints who sometimes sin. It's important to recognize our failures, confess them to God, and receive His forgiveness. The person who deceives himself by ignoring his sinful acts and allowing them to build up is headed for a great fall.

Those of us who live in earthquake-prone Southern California keep hearing about "the big one," which many experts think is coming. Whenever we experience minor earthquakes, we may be frightened by them a bit, but we also see them as a good sign. These little shakes mean that the plates in the earth's crust beneath us are shifting. As long as the crust is adjusting this way it's unlikely that "the big one" will hit. It's when we don't get any minor earthquakes for several months or years that the danger of a major, devastating quake increases.

When we live in obedience to God's Word and deal with our sin on a daily basis, we prevent the major spiritual earthquakes from building up in our lives. If we keep saying, "I don't have any sin," or if we fail to admit our failures as God convicts us of them, we're in for "the big one."

We deceive ourselves when we think we are better than we are (Romans 12:3; Galatians 6:3). "But I know who I am," we say. "I'm a child of God, I'm seated with Christ, I can do all things through Him. That makes me pretty special." Yes, we are very special in the eyes of God. But we are what we are by the grace of God (1 Corinthians 15:10). The life we live, the talents we possess, and the gifts we have received are not personal accomplishments; they are expressions of God's grace. We must never take credit for what God has provided. Rather, we must find joy in doing things that glorify the Lord.

We deceive ourselves when we think we are smarter than we are (1 Corinthians 3:18,19). Sometimes we are tempted to think we are as smart as Satan, the god of this world. But we are no match for him. Whenever we think we can outsmart Satan on our own, we become a prime target to be hit by one of his crafty tricks.

However, Satan is no match for God. It is important for us not to lean on our own understanding, but to use the mind of Christ and put Him first in all our ways (Proverbs 3:5,6; 1 Corinthians 2:16).

We deceive ourselves when we think we are good Christians but do not control our speech (James 1:26). There is nothing that saddens God more than when we bad-mouth others instead of building them up with our speech. We are never to use our tongues to put others down. Instead we are to build each other up in what we say. If our speech is out of control, we're fooling ourselves to believe that we have our spiritual life together.

We deceive ourselves when we think our sin will not lead to consequences (Galatians 6:7). As Christians we sometimes think we have special privileges so that our sins won't have any bad effects. But we have to live with the results and consequences of our thoughts, words, and actions, just like unbelievers.

We deceive ourselves when we think people living totally in sin are Christians (1 Corinthians 6:9,10). Kate, a coworker of mine (Neil), walked into the office one day completely devastated. She had just learned that her older sister, who had led her to Christ, had walked away from God and was living in a lesbian relationship. "My lifestyle doesn't make any difference," Kate's sister had argued. "God loves me and I'm forgiven." Kate was distraught and confused.

I showed her 1 Corinthians 6:9,10: "Don't fool yourselves. Those who live immoral lives, who are idol worshipers, adulterers or homosexuals—will have no share in [God's] kingdom" (TLB). Kate's sister and others like her are deceived. Living a consistently sinful life is strong evidence that a person is not in right relationship with God. We are absolutely deceived if we believe that our walk doesn't have to line up with our talk.

We deceive ourselves when we think we can always hang out with bad people and not be influenced by them (1 Corinthians 15:33). My (Dave) brother-in-law was raised in a strong and loving Christian home, so he thought he could hang out with ungodly people and not be affected. But he was enticed so far from his values that he actually became part of a vicious hate group called the skinheads.

Does this mean that we shouldn't minister to those with bad morals? No, we must share Christ with them. But if we spend all our time on their turf, our ministry will eventually dry up and our morality will be affected for the worse.

Beware of False Prophets and Teachers

Alvin was discouraged and defeated. He came to see me (Neil) because for several years he believed he had a special gift of prophecy from God. But over a period of months his personal life began to fall apart. Alvin eventually reached the point where he began to withdraw from people completely. He was a slave to prescription drugs and had checked out of society.

Alvin and I read 1 Thessalonians 5:19-21: "Do not put out the Spirit's fire; do not treat prophecies with contempt. Test everything. Hold on to the good" (NIV). I said, "Alvin, I'm not against prophecy; it's a spiritual gift. But Satan can produce fake spiritual gifts and deceive us into believing they're from God. That's why the Scriptures instruct us to put everything to the test."

After a lengthy discussion about false prophets and teachers, Alvin admitted, "I think my problems began when I failed to test the 'gifts' of tongues and prophecy given to me by false teachers. Not only was I deceived, but I have deceived others myself."

"Would you be willing to put your gift of tongues to the test?" I asked. I assured Alvin that I was interested in testing the spirit, not him.

Alvin really wanted to be free of deception and right with God. "Yes," he answered.

I asked Alvin to begin praying aloud in his "spiritual language." As he began to chant in a language I couldn't understand, I said, "In the name of Christ and in obedience to God's Word, I command you, spirit, to identify yourself."

Alvin stopped in the middle of his chanting and said, "I am he."

"Are you the 'he' who was crucified, buried, raised on the third day, and who now sits at the right hand of the Father?" I continued.

Alvin almost shouted the response: "No! Not he!" I led Alvin through a prayer renouncing Satan's activity in his life, and he was free from that deception.

We're not against spiritual gifts, even prophecy and tongues. We are, however, committed to obeying Scripture. First Corinthians 14:39 says, "Desire earnestly to prophesy, and do not forbid to speak in tongues." But Scripture also requires that all spiritual gifts be tested. False prophets and teachers are popular everywhere today simply because Christians accept their ministry without testing the spirits behind it.

Comparing the Phony with the Real

In Jeremiah 23, the Lord revealed through His prophet several qualifications for a true prophet from God.

A true prophet brings people to God (verses 16,21,22). Every true prophet of God in the Old Testament was an evangelist. The prophet's ministry drew people back to God and His Word. If you come across someone who claims to be a prophet, but who is not involved in calling people to a righteous walk with God, you may be dealing with a phony.

A true prophet's dreams agree with God's Word (verses 25,28). God often spoke to people in the Bible through the dreams of godly people. In these verses God compares dreams to straw and His Word to grain. If you feed straw to cattle, they'll die. They will sleep on it, but they won't eat it because it has no nutrients. In the same way, dreams are of some value, but they are never to be made equal to God's Word as the basis for our faith or our walk. Dreams must be checked out against God's Word; it's never the other way around.

A true prophet's message moves people to get right with God (verse 29). Jeremiah writes: "'Is not my word like fire?' declares the LORD, 'and like a hammer which shatters a rock?'" If you attend a youth group meeting or church where prophecies are part of the worship service, don't expect from God sugar-sweet messages like, "I love you, My children" or "I'm coming soon." These statements are certainly true. But why would they need to be prophesied, since the Bible clearly states God's love and Christ's soon return?

The voice of a prophet should be like a consuming fire and a shattering hammer. A prophetic message should motivate people to righteousness, not leave them comfortable in their sin (1 Peter 4:17).

The true prophet gets his message from God, not from other people (verses 30,31). Taking what God gave someone else and using it as if it were your own is called plagiarism—stealing someone else's ideas. Also, declaring that what you are saying is directly from the Lord when it isn't is an incredible slam against God. Has anybody ever come up to you and said, "The Lord told me to tell you . . . "? You can respond, "No, I don't believe He did! If God wants me to know something He can tell me directly."

God can and will encourage us and confirm His Word to us through others. But when it comes to receiving direction for our life, "there is one God, and one mediator also between God and men, the man Christ Jesus" (1 Timothy 2:5). If someone says to you, "God told me to tell you . . . ," that person may be acting as a spiritual medium. And listening to a medium is forbidden in the Bible.

Signs and Wonders: Who's Being Tested?

Many young Christians think that if a person can perform a miracle, he must be doing it with God's power. God can still use signs and wonders to show that His Word is true, but the Bible also warns that "there will be many false Messiahs and false prophets who will do wonderful miracles that would deceive, if possible, even God's own children" (Mark 13:22 TLB). Satan can also perform signs and wonders, but he only does so to direct our worship away from God to himself.

Deuteronomy 13:5-11 reveals the seriousness of attributing to God the activity of Satan. Persons who were involved in it were to be killed, even if they were relatives. We are to love God, obey His Word, and test all signs, wonders, and dreams.

Counterfeits in the Church

False prophets and false teachers are not just Eastern mystics and gurus and non-Christian cult leaders. The apostle Peter devoted an entire chapter in one of his letters to false prophets and teachers who work *within* the church: "There will also be false teachers among you, who will secretly introduce destructive heresies, even denying the Master who bought them, bringing swift destruction upon themselves" (2 Peter 2:1). These people are in our churches right now, disguised as Christian leaders.

Notice that the attraction of false teachers is not primarily their doctrine: "And many will follow their sensuality" (verse 2). Peter is talking about Christians who evaluate a ministry based on the outward appearance and charm of its leaders. We say, "He's such a nice guy"; "She's a very charismatic person"; "He's a real dynamic speaker"; "She's so sweet and sounds so sincere."

But we are never to judge a ministry or its leaders on the basis of physical appearance or personality. The important issue is whether or not the person proclaims God's Word as the truth and calls people to get right with God through faith in Jesus Christ.

Peter goes on to reveal two ways we can identify false prophets and false teachers in the church. First, they will be involved in immorality of some kind (verse 10). They may be discovered in illegal and immoral activities involving sex and/or money. They may claim that God is full of love and grace, so we don't need to obey any moral laws. Their immorality may not be easy to spot, but it will eventually surface in their lives (2 Corinthians 11:15).

Second, false prophets and teachers "despise authority" and are "daring, self-willed" (2 Peter 2:10). These people do their own thing and won't answer to anybody. They either won't submit to the authority of those over them, or they will pick their own so-called leaders who will always agree with anything they want to do. Every true, committed Christian in a leadership role needs to submit himself and his ideas to other mature believers who will hold him accountable.

Beware of Deceiving Spirits

In addition to warning us against self-deception and false prophets and teachers, the Bible warns us against the deception which comes through demonic influence. Paul alerted Timothy: "The Spirit explicitly says that in later times some will fall away from the faith, paying attention to deceitful spirits and doctrines of demons" (1 Timothy 4:1). John also cautioned us to test the spirits in order to know the difference between the spirit of truth and the spirit of error (1 John 4:1-6).

I (Dave) was reminded of the deception of evil spirits among young people when I talked to a girl named Ashley at a junior high camp in Missouri. "I'm being visited by my dead sister, Brandy," she blurted out.

"Tell me what's happening," I said.

"After my sister died, my mother used to go visit Brandy's grave. Mom said Brandy would talk with her there for hours. Soon Mom said she could see Brandy, who rode part of the way home with her in the car. Eventually Brandy was visiting my mother at our home. Now even I can see her and talk to her."

I turned to Luke 16 in my Bible and asked Ashley to read aloud the story about the rich man and Lazarus (verses 19-26). Then I asked her to read verse 26 a second time, the words of Abraham in heaven to the rich man in hell. Ashley read, "Between us and you there is a great chasm fixed, in order that those who wish to come over from here to you may not be able, and that none may cross over from there to us."

I said, "According to these verses, is the person visiting you and your mother really your sister?"

"No," she answered quickly, "it can't be, can it? No one can return from the dead."

"That's right, Ashley."

"But it looks and sounds exactly like her!"

"That's just part of Satan's deception. His demons are so evil and low that they will even impersonate a precious loved one to try to lead you away from God and His Word."

Ashley nodded. "I realize now that this thing is not my sister and it's not from God."

While Ashley's experience is becoming more common among young people, Satan will probably try to influence our minds rather than appear to us. Satan's demonic forces are at work trying to pollute our minds with lies in order to keep us from walking in the truth.

The following is an example of the kind of prayer we need to pray in order to keep ourselves from deceiving spirits:

> Heavenly Father, I commit myself totally to Your will. If I have been deceived in any way, I pray that You will open my eyes to the deception. I command in the name of the Lord Jesus Christ that all deceiving spirits

depart from me. I reject all phony spiritual gifts or happenings. Lord, bless anything that is from You and cause it to grow that Your body may be blessed and built up through it. Amen.

Discerning Deception

Our first line of defense against Satan's deception is discernment. Discernment is that buzzer that sounds inside you warning that something is wrong. Discernment simply means to make a judgment or a distinction. It has only one purpose: to distinguish right from wrong so the right can be encouraged and the wrong can be eliminated. In 1 Corinthians 12:10 discernment is the God-given ability to distinguish a good spirit from a bad spirit. It is one of the gifts of the Spirit which is to be used to build up the church.

Discernment is not an act of the mind; it's an act of the Holy Spirit, who dwells within us. When the Spirit sounds a warning, your mind, which is designed to deal with facts, may not be able to understand what's wrong. But when you discern that something is wrong, you don't need to understand it to act on the warning. Simply say to those with you, "I sense that something is out of order here. Let's ask God to help us." Then allow God to bring the problem to light as only He can.

We are more vulnerable to Satan's deception than to any of his other schemes. Why? Because when he tempts us or accuses us, we know it. But when he deceives us, we don't know it. That's his strategy: to keep us in the dark. If he can get into our youth groups, our homes, and our minds without being noticed, he can control those areas. Sadly, he is doing just that across our land by deceiving many people.

You cannot expose Satan's deception by human reasoning; you can only do it by God's revelation. Jesus said, "If you abide in My word, then you are truly disciples of Mine; and you shall know the truth, and the truth shall make you free" (John 8:31,32). Jesus prayed, "Sanctify them [keep them from evil] in the truth; Thy word is truth" (John 17:17).

When you put on the armor of God, it is important that you start with the belt of truth (Ephesians 6:14). The light of truth is the only valid weapon against the darkness of deception.

Here is an encouraging letter from a young girl who was trapped in deception until the Bondage Breaker set her free:

Dear Dr. Anderson:

I will always remember the day I came to you for counsel and prayer. Ever since that day I have felt such freedom. There are no more voices or feelings of heaviness in my brain. I'm even enjoying a physical sense of release. Satan has returned many times trying to clobber me with those old thoughts, but his hold on me has been broken.

I'll never forget what you told me. You said that those negative thoughts about God and myself were lies that Satan planted in my mind. You said I have the power through Jesus Christ to rebuke Satan and get rid of the evil thoughts. It has taken me awhile to really believe that with all my heart, but lately I've decided to fight back—and it works! It's been wonderful to deal with my problems with a clear head. Thank you for helping me and so many others find peace and learn to trust, love, and believe in the Lord.

Love in Christ

Truth Encounter

Read: James 4:7; Jeremiah 23:16-31

Reflect: 1. Do you have any Christian friends that seem to be defeated and deceived like the girl Alyce in this chapter? Is there hope for people who find themselves in bondage to Satan's lies? What is that hope?

2. In this chapter we talked a lot about self-deceptions. Which of these deceptions do you think is most common among Christian young people today? Which self-deception do you struggle with most?

3. What are some of the signs of a genuine prophet? Why should Christian leaders be accountable to other leaders in their ministry?

4. How can a false prophet be identified? Why is understanding God's Word so important when it comes to spotting a false prophet?

Respond: Review the list of self-deceptions that are talked about in this chapter. Pray through each deception and ask God to reveal if you have knowingly or unknowingly become deceived in any of the areas talked about. Whatever God brings to mind, deal with it by first confessing the deception, then renouncing your involvement.

11

The Danger of Losing Control

I received the following letter from a young woman I have never met. Sheila attended one of our conferences and wrote:

Dear Neil,

I have been set free—praise the Lord! Yesterday, for the first time in years, the voices stopped. I could hear the silence. When we sang, I could hear myself sing.

For the first 14 years of my life I lived with an oppressive, abusive mother who never said, "I love you," or put her arms around me when I cried. I received no affection, no kind words, no affirmation, no sense of who I was—only physical and emotional abuse. At 15 I was subjected to three weeks of Erhard Seminar Training (EST), which really screwed up my mind. The year which followed was pure hell.

My mother threw me out, so I went to live with another family. Eventually they also threw me out.

Three years later I found Christ. My decision to trust Christ was largely based on my fear of Satan and the power of evil I had experienced in my life. Even though I knew Satan had lost his ownership of me, I was unaware of how vulnerable I still was to his deception and control. For the first two years of my Christian life I was in bondage to a sin I didn't even know was a sin. Once I realized my sin, confessed it to God, and received forgiveness, I thought I was finally free of Satan's attempts to control me. I didn't realize that the battle had only begun.

I suffered from unexplainable rashes, hives, and welts all over my body. I lost my joy and closeness to the Lord. I could no longer sing or quote Scripture. I turned to food as my comfort and security. The demons attacked my sense of right and wrong, and I became involved in immorality in my search for identity and love.

But that all ended yesterday when I renounced Satan's control in my life. I have found the freedom and protection which comes from knowing I am loved. I'm not on a high. I'm writing with a clear mind, a clean spirit, and a calm hand. Even my previous bondage to food seems suddenly foreign to me.

I never realized that a Christian could be so vulnerable to Satan's control. I was deceived, but now I am free. Thank You, thank You, Jesus!

Sheila

Sheila is a sobering example of a level of spiritual attack that most Christians don't like to talk about: demonic control. As a believer, Sheila had lost control in her eating habits, in her sexual behavior, and in her devotional life. She wasn't growing spiritually; she was shrinking. She didn't sing and read Scripture because she was blocked from doing so.

Most of us agree that Christians are clear targets for the enemy's temptation, accusation, and deception. But for some reason we hesitate to admit that Christians can lose their freedom and can surrender to demonic influences. However, there is much clear evidence in Scripture that believers who repeatedly give in to temptation, accusation, and deception can fall back into bondage to sin.

Thankfully, demonic *bondage* does not mean satanic *ownership*. Like Sheila, we have been purchased by the blood of the Lamb, and not even the powers of hell can take our salvation away from us (1 Peter 1:17-19; Romans 8:35-39). Satan knows he can never own us again. But if he can deceive us into surrendering control of our life to him in some way, he can hinder our growth and our impact in the world for Christ. Since we live in a world whose god is Satan, the possibility of being tempted, deceived, and accused is continuous. If we allow his schemes to influence us, we can lose control to the level that we have been deceived.

Demonic Control of the Saints

It is very important that we understand that Christians are the targets for demonic influence. Those who say a demon cannot affect a believer's life have left us with only two possible answers for the problems we face: Either we are the cause or God is. If we blame ourselves we feel hopeless because we can't do anything to stop what we're doing. If we blame God our confidence in Him as our loving Father is shattered. Either way, we have no chance to gain the victory which the Bible promises us.

In reality we are in a winnable war against demonic powers from the defeated kingdom of darkness. If Satan can get you to believe a lie, he can control your life.

Here are several indications from the Bible that believers can come under bondage to demonic influence.

Luke 13:10-18. While Jesus was teaching in the synagogue (the Jewish place of worship and study), "there was a woman who for eighteen years had had a sickness caused by a spirit; and she was bent double, and could not straighten up at all" (verse 11). Verse 16 states that her physical disability was caused by satanic bondage. This woman was not an unbeliever. She was a God-fearing woman of faith with a spiritual problem. As soon as Jesus released her from bondage, her physical problem was cured.

Notice that this woman wasn't protected from demonic control by being inside the synagogue. The walls of a church can't protect us from demonic influence either. If plaster walls are not a barrier to Satan, do you think your skin is? The spiritual world is not subject to such natural barriers.

Yes, this event occurred before the cross. But it is an indication that believers can be physically affected by demons.

Luke 22:31-34. The apostle Peter is an example of a believer who temporarily lost control to Satan. Jesus said to him, "Simon, Simon, behold, Satan has demanded permission to sift you like wheat" (verse 31). What right did Satan have to make such a demand? Peter had apparently given Satan an open door through pride when he debated with the disciples about which of them was the greatest (Luke 22:24). Even though Peter wholeheartedly intended to stand by his Master to the death (verse 33), Jesus announced that Peter would deny Him three times (verse 34), which he did. It's encouraging to know that Jesus had already prayed for Peter's successful recovery (verse 32).

Ephesians 6:10-17. These verses contain Paul's strong encouragement to believers to "put on the full armor of God, that you may be able to stand firm against the schemes of the devil" (verse 11). What is the purpose of armor? To prevent the enemy's arrows from penetrating the body and injuring the soldier. If it is impossible for Satan's arrows to penetrate us, there would be no need for us to put on the armor. Paul's teaching about spiritual armor suggests that it is possible for the enemy to penetrate our lives and gain a measure of control.

James 3:14-16. James tells us that if we yield to jealousy and selfish ambition, we may open ourselves to being controlled by wisdom which is "earthly, natural, demonic" (verse 15).

1 Timothy 4:1-3. Paul wrote, "Some will fall away from the faith, paying attention to deceitful spirits and doctrines of demons" (verse 1). Satan can deceive your mind where you are vulnerable to his control. Evidences of control mentioned here are unbiblical practices in the areas of eating habits and marriage (verse 3).

1 Corinthians 5:1-13. This passage contains Paul's teaching about a Christian man who was living with his father's wife (verse 1). He was a man so deceived by Satan and controlled by immorality that he apparently bragged about his sinful relationship in front of the whole church. Paul's judgment on the matter was severe: "I have decided to deliver such a one to Satan for the destruction of his flesh, that his spirit may be saved in the day of the Lord Jesus" (verse 5). Paul let Satan have his way with the man for awhile in hopes that he would finally say "I've had enough" and repent.

Some people wonder if a person living this deeply in sin is really a Christian. But if this man were a non-Christian, Paul would not have corrected him, because the church is only required to discipline its members, not unbelievers. This man was a believer (at least Paul treated him like one) who had allowed himself to become trapped in sexual sin. Paul's hope was that he experience the natural consequences of his sin, repent, and be set free from his bondage.

Ephesians 4:26,27. Paul instructed, "'In your anger do not sin': Do not let the sun go down while you are still angry, and do not give the devil a foothold" (NIV). The word *foothold* literally means a "place." Paul is saying that we may give the devil a place in our lives if we fail to speak the truth in love and manage our emotions. Anger which turns to bitterness and unforgiveness is an open door for Satan (2 Corinthians 2:10,11).

1 Peter 5:6-9. Peter warned, "Your adversary, the devil, prowls about like a roaring lion, seeking someone to devour" (verse 8). The word *devour* means to swallow up. To be swallowed up by something certainly conveys the thought of being controlled by it. If believers can't be controlled by Satan, Peter would not need to warn us about the possibility.

Peter's warning suggests two conditions which may open up a believer to Satan's control. In verse 6 we are encouraged to humble ourselves before the Lord. Peter indicates that whenever we resist pride we resist Satan. And verses 7 and 8 suggest that if we don't learn how to cast our worries on the Lord, we make ourselves easy prey.

Acts 5:1-11. The members of the young Jerusalem church were freely selling their property and giving the profits to the apostles for use in ministry. "But a certain man named Ananias, with his wife Sapphira, sold a piece of property, and kept back some of the price for himself, with his wife's full knowledge, and bringing a portion of it, he laid it at the apostles' feet. But Peter said, 'Ananias, why has Satan filled your

heart to lie to the Holy Spirit, and to keep back some of
the price of the land? . . . You have not lied to men, but
to God'" (verses 1-4).

The problem was not that Ananias and Sapphira
kept part of the money but that they lied about it. They
apparently said that what they gave was the total
amount they received. The consequence of the couple's
sin was immediate and sobering: They died on the
spot (verses 5,10).

This event took place inside the Christian church,
and Ananias and Sapphira were obviously members.
Why did God so dramatically judge Ananias and Sapphira in the struggling early days of the church?
Because He knew what the real battle was going to be
for the church. If Satan can get into your church, your
home, or you undetected, and convince you to believe
a lie, he can control your life.

Acts 5:11 says, "And great fear came upon the
whole church." If God were judging someone *outside*
the church, why would great fear come upon those
inside the church? There was great fear among *believers*
because God had dramatically displayed what He
thinks about *believers* who live a lie.

The tough punishment showed that God was
emphasizing the importance of truth in the community of believers. Unbelievers lie all the time, but they
aren't zapped dead like Ananias and Sapphira were.
God was communicating early in the church's history
that our major problem is not drugs, sex, or false religions; it's giving in to Satan's deception.

Ananias' problem was that he had allowed Satan's
deception to fill (control) his heart. The word *filled* in
Acts 5:3 is the same word used in Ephesians 5:18: "Be

filled with the Spirit." It is possible for believers to be filled with satanic deception or filled by the Spirit. To whichever source we yield, by that source we shall be filled and controlled. When we allow Satan to deceive us in any area of our life, we are open to his control in that area.

Responsibility for Resisting Control

We can't totally blame Ananias and Sapphira's fall on Satan. We must remember that these two believers willingly participated in the lie which led to their deaths. Peter asked them individually: "Why is it that you have conceived this deed in your heart?"; "Why is it that you have agreed together to put the Spirit of the Lord to the test?" (Acts 5:4,9). Yes, Satan filled their hearts with deception and exercised a measure of control over them in their sin. But he was only able to do so because at some point Ananias and Sapphira opened the door for him.

Don't ever believe someone who says, "The devil made me do it." No, he didn't make us do it; *we* allowed him to do it. Somewhere along the line we chose to give the devil a foothold. He merely took advantage of the opportunity we gave him. We have all the resources and protection we need to live a victorious life in Christ every day. If we're not living it, it's our choice. When we leave a door open for the devil by not resisting temptation, accusation, or deception, he will enter it. And if we continue to allow him access to that area, he will eventually control it. We won't lose our salvation, but we will lose our daily victory.

Many young Christians today who cannot control their lives in some area sit around blaming themselves instead of solving the problem. They scold themselves and punish themselves for not having the willpower to break a bad habit when instead they should be resisting Satan in an area where he has robbed them of control. Anything bad which you cannot stop doing, or anything good which you cannot make yourself do, is an area of bondage.

If We're Not Responsible, We Will Lose Control

In Chapter 5 we looked at the believer's protection in the face of demonic attack. We must assume our responsibility. This protection is not something we can take for granted. God's protection depends on our willingness to apply the protection God has provided.

In Romans 13:14 we are told to "put on the Lord Jesus Christ, and make no provision for the flesh in regard to its lusts." But what if we *do* make provision for the flesh by giving Satan an opening in our life through sin? Do we have unlimited protection from Satan's invasion no matter what we do? No, we must do what God tells us to do to take advantage of His protection.

James 4:7 tells us to "resist the devil and he will flee from you." What if we don't resist him? Is he required to run from us if we don't take our stand against him? No, if we don't resist him, he doesn't have to go. God's protection in this area is guaranteed, but we switch on that protection by resisting Satan.

Ephesians 6:10-17 describes the armor of God which we are instructed to put on in order to "stand firm against the schemes of the devil" (verse 11). But if we go into battle without our armor, will God protect us from getting wounded? No, if we fail to cover ourselves with the armor God has provided, we are vulnerable in those exposed areas.

James 4:1 tells us that the source of our quarrels and fights is the evil desires within us. Paul instructed, "Do not let sin control your puny body any longer; do not give in to its sinful desires" (Romans 6:12 TLB). The world, the flesh, and the devil are continually at war against the life of the Spirit within us. But what if we don't fight back? Will we still be victorious over the evil desires that try to rule over us? No, they will control us if we fail to halt their invasion by resisting Satan.

Choosing truth, living a righteous life, and putting on the armor of God is each believer's individual responsibility. Mom and Dad, your pastor, and your youth leader are not responsible for you. They can pray for you, encourage you in the faith, and support you. But if you go into the battle without your armor on, you may get hurt. Those who love you may be very concerned for you, but they still can't make those decisions of responsibility for you. Those choices are yours alone.

At this point you may be thinking like the apostle Paul in Romans 7:15, "I am not practicing what I would like to do, but I am doing the very thing I hate." You realize that you have been a target for Satan's temptation, accusation, and deception. You haven't been resisting Satan as you should. You wonder, "Am I stuck in my problems? I have left the door open for Satan, and he has taken advantage of me. Can I get him out of the places he has wormed into?"

The answer is yes! Jesus Christ is the Bondage Breaker. But in order to experience His freedom, we must find the doors we left open through which Satan gained entrance. We must say, "Lord, I confess that I am responsible for giving Satan a foothold in my life, and I renounce the involvement with him which has led to my bondage." We call this process the *steps to freedom.* Are you ready to be free? Chapter 12 will lead you through the biblical steps to freedom, and then you will be free indeed.

Truth Encounter

Read: Romans 13:4; Ephesians 6:10-17; Romans 6:12

Reflect: 1. In this chapter we gave some biblical examples of saints who lost control and allowed the enemy to influence them. How was the apostle Peter deceived? (For help, see Luke 22:31-34.)

2. In what way did Satan deceive Ananias and Sapphira? What main issue was God concerned about? (For help, see Acts 5:1-11.)

3. What insights did you gain that will help you stay free from any demonic deceptions or control?

4. What protection has God given us against Satan's deceptions and control?

Respond: Pray and ask God to reveal to your mind any time in which you might have surrendered to Satan's deception and failed to resist Satan, failed to put on God's armor, or let sin reign in your life. Be sure to confess and renounce any event that comes to mind.

PART THREE

Walk Free!

12

Steps to Freedom in Christ

If you have received Christ as your personal Savior, He has set you free from sin and Satan's power through His victory on the cross and His resurrection. But if you are not *experiencing* freedom in your daily life, it may be because you have not realized who you are in Christ and taken a stand against the devil and his lies. It is your responsibility to do whatever is necessary to maintain a right relationship with God. Your eternal relationship with God is not at stake; you are safe and secure in Christ. But your daily victory in Him will be shaky at best if you fail to claim and maintain your freedom.

In this chapter we want to present seven steps you need to take in order to experience the full freedom and victory that Christ purchased for you on the cross. Don't expect someone else to take these steps for you. This is something you alone must do, even though we strongly recommend that a mature Christian sit with you as you go through these steps (a parent, a trusted friend, a pastor or youth leader,

a counselor, etc.). Your freedom will be the result of
what you choose to believe, confess, forgive, renounce, and forsake. No one can believe for you.
The battle for your mind can only be won as you
personally choose truth.

As you go through these steps, you may experience thoughts like, "This isn't going to work" or
"God doesn't love me." Those are lies from the
enemy. They can only stop you if you believe them.
If you are working through these steps alone, don't
pay attention to Satan's lies. If another Christian is
working with you as we recommend, share with
that person any thoughts which tempt you to give
up. As soon as you uncover the lie, the power of
Satan is broken.

Remember that Satan will be defeated only if you
confront him aloud. He doesn't have to obey your
thoughts. Only God perfectly knows what is going
on in your mind. As you take each step, it is important that you submit to God in your heart and then
resist the devil by reading aloud each prayer and
statement (James 4:7).

Here is a prayer to get you started. Pray it out
loud from your heart:

> Dear heavenly Father, I know that You
> are here in this room and present in my
> life. You are the only all-knowing, all-
> powerful, ever-present God. I desperately
> need You, because without Jesus I can do
> nothing. I believe the Bible because it tells
> me what is really true. I refuse to believe
> the lies of Satan. I stand in the truth that all
> authority in heaven and on earth has been

given to the risen Christ. I ask You to protect my thoughts and mind, to fill me with Your Holy Spirit, and to lead me into all truth. I pray for Your complete protection. In Jesus' name I pray. Amen.

If a Christian friend or counselor is with you, he or she may declare the following for you, or declare it for yourself aloud:

In the name and the authority of the Lord Jesus Christ, we command Satan and all evil spirits to let go of (name) in order that (name) can be free to know and choose to do the will of God. As children of God seated with Christ in the heavenlies, we agree that every enemy of the Lord Jesus Christ be bound and gagged to silence in (name). We say to Satan and all of his evil workers that you cannot inflict any pain or in any way stop or hinder God's will from being done today in (name).

Step 1:
Counterfeit Versus Real

The first step to freedom in Christ is to renounce (turn your back on) any present or past involvement with satanically inspired occult practices or false religions. You must renounce any activity and group which denies Jesus Christ, tries to direct your life through any source other than the Bible, or requires secret initiations, ceremonies, promises, or pacts (covenants). No Christian has any business being part of a group that is not completely open about what they do (1 John 1:5,7).

You must not only choose truth but reject Satan and his lies. There is no middle ground. Jesus said, "He who is not with Me is against Me" (Luke 11:23). There are not many paths to God; there is only one way (John 14:6). Other religions and cults may talk about Jesus, but they present Him in another way than He is presented in the Bible. They may agree that Jesus lived in history but fail to call Him the Son of God.

In order to help you evaluate the spiritual experiences of your life, fill out the "Non-Christian Spiritual Checklist" (pp. 189-190). The list will help you identify any non-Christian practices you have been involved in. If the list does not include something you have done which you feel was a non-Christian practice, be sure to add it. Even if you were "innocently" involved in something, or only watched someone else who was involved, you should write it on your list and renounce it just in case you gave Satan a foothold without realizing it.

Don't be surprised if you feel some resistance as you complete this step. Satan doesn't want you to be free, and he will do whatever he can do to keep you from claiming your freedom.

As you go through this step, pray in the following way:

> Dear heavenly Father, I ask You to reveal to me anything that I have done or that someone has done to me that is spiritually wrong. Show me how I have been involved with any cults, false religions, occult/satanic practices, or false teachers, whether I knew I

was involved or not. I want to experience Your freedom and do Your will. I ask this in Jesus' name. Amen.

Non-Christian Spiritual Checklist

Circle any of the following activities in which you have been involved in any way.

OCCULT
out-of-body experience
Ouija board
Bloody Mary
Magic Eight Ball
table lifting or body lifting
using spells or curses
automatic writing
spirit guides
fortune-telling
tarot cards
palm-reading
astrology/horoscopes
hypnosis
seances
black or white magic
Dungeons & Dragons
other fantasy games
blood pacts or cutting your-
    self in a destructive way
objects of worship, crystals,
    or good luck charms
others:

CULT
Mormonism
Jehovah's Witnesses
New Age
New Age medicine
Masons
Scientology
Christian Science
others:

OTHER RELIGIONS
Zen Buddhism
Hinduism
Islam
martial arts
transcendental meditation
yoga
others:

Write down the titles of any anti-Christian movies, music, books, magazines, comic books, TV programs, video games, etc. which may have influenced you in a wrong way.

movies:

music:

books, magazines, comic books:

TV programs, video games:

1. Have you ever felt, heard, or seen a spiritual being in your room?

2. Have you had an imaginary friend who talks to you?

3. Have you ever heard voices in your head or had repeating, nagging thoughts like, "I'm dumb," "I'm ugly," "I can't do anything right," etc., as if there were a conversation going on in your head?

4. Have you or anyone in your family ever consulted a medium, spiritist, or channeler?

5. What other spiritual experiences have you had that could be considered out of the ordinary (telepathy, speaking in a trance, knowing something supernaturally, etc.)?

6. Have you ever been involved in satanic worship of any form or attended a concert where Satan was the focus?

When you are sure that your list is complete, confess and renounce each involvement by praying aloud the following prayer, repeating it separately for each item on your list:

> Lord, I confess that I have participated in
> _____. I ask Your forgiveness, and I
> renounce _____ as a counterfeit to
> true Christianity.

Have you been involved in satanic rituals or heavy occult activity? Or have you experienced severe nightmares, suggesting that satanic, occult activity in your past has been blocked from your memory? All satanic rituals, covenants (promises), and assignments must be specifically renounced as the Lord allows you to remember them.

Step 2:
Deception Versus Truth

The truth is found in God's Word, the Bible. God desires us to plant His truth in our hearts so we live the truth (Psalm 51:6). When David lived a lie he really suffered. When he finally found freedom by agreeing with the truth, he wrote, "How blessed is the man . . .

in whose spirit there is no deceit" (Psalm 32:2). We must get rid of anything false in our lives and speak the truth in love (Ephesians 4:15,25).

Begin this important step by reading aloud the following prayer:

> Dear heavenly Father, I know that You want me to face the truth and that I must be honest with You. I know that choosing to believe the truth will set me free (John 8:32). I have been deceived by Satan, the father of lies (John 8:44), and I have deceived myself (1 John 1:8). I thought I could hide it from You, but You see everything and still love me. I pray in the name of the Lord Jesus Christ, asking You to rebuke all of Satan's demons through Your righteous Son Jesus, who shed His blood on the cross and rose from the dead for me. I have asked Jesus into my life, and I am Your child. Therefore, by the authority of the Lord Jesus Christ I command all evil spirits to leave me. I ask the Holy Spirit to lead me into all truth. I ask You to look deep inside me and know my heart. Show me if there is anything in me that I am trying to hide (Psalm 139:23,24), because I want to be free. In Jesus' name I pray. Amen.

You may want to take some time at this point to think of the evil tricks Satan has used to deceive you. Have you been listening to false teachers or deceiving spirits? Have you been living under self-deception? Have you used excuses to defend your behavior? Now that you are alive in Christ and forgiven, you don't have to live a lie, and you don't have to defend your-self! Check those below that apply to you:

How You Can Deceive Yourself

_____ Hear God's Word but not do it (James 1:22; 4:17)

_____ Say you have no sin (1 John 1:8)

_____ Think you are something you are really not (Galatians 6:3)

_____ Think you are wise in the things of the world (1 Corinthians 3:18,19)

_____ Think you will not reap what you sow (Galatians 6:7)

_____ Think that unholy people will share in God's kingdom (1 Corinthians 6:9)

_____ Think you can be with bad company and it won't have any influence on you (1 Corinthians 15:33)

Wrong Ways to Defend Yourself

_____ Refuse to face the real things that have happened to you

_____ Escape from the real world

_____ Withdraw to avoid rejection

_____ Revert to a less threatening time

_____ Take out frustrations on others

_____ Blame others

_____ Look for an excuse

For those things that have been true in your life, pray aloud:

> Lord, I agree that I have been deceived in the area of _____. Thank You for forgiving me. I commit myself to know and follow Your truth.

Choosing truth may be difficult if you have been living a lie (been deceived) for some time. Knowing that you are forgiven and accepted as God's child is what sets you free to face reality and declare your dependence on Him.

Faith is God's way for us to respond to the truth, and believing the truth is a choice. When someone says, "I want to believe God, but I just can't," they are being deceived. Of course we can believe God! Faith is something you decide to do, not something you feel like doing. Believing the truth doesn't make it true. It's true, so we believe it.

It's not the idea that we "believe" something that's important; it's what or who we believe in. Everybody believes in something, and everybody walks by faith according to what they believe. But if what we believe isn't true, then how we live won't be right.

It is very important for Christians to declare what they believe based on the truth of God's Word. Filling our minds and hearts with the truth is the best way to free ourselves of Satan's deception. Read aloud the following "Statement of Truth." Read it every day for several weeks in order to renew your mind and build your faith.

Statement of Truth

1. I believe that there is only one true and living God (Exodus 20:2,3) who exists as the Father, Son, and

Holy Spirit. He alone is worthy of all honor, praise, and glory. I believe that He made all things and holds all things together (Colossians 1:16,17).

2. I recognize Jesus Christ as the Messiah, the Word who became flesh and lived with us (John 1:1,14). I believe that He came to destroy the works of Satan (1 John 3:8).

3. I believe that God showed how much He loves me by sending Christ to die for me even though I was sinful (Romans 5:8). I believe that God rescued me from the kingdom of darkness and brought me into the kingdom of His Son, who has forgiven my sins and set me free (Colossians 1:13,14).

4. I believe I am spiritually strong because Jesus is my strength. I have the authority to stand against Satan because I am a child of God (1 John 3:1-3). I believe that I was saved by the grace of God through faith, that it was a gift and not the result of any works on my part (Ephesians 2:8).

5. I choose to be strong in the Lord and in the strength of His might (Ephesians 6:10). I put no confidence in the flesh (Philippians 3:3) for the weapons of our warfare are not of the flesh (2 Corinthians 10:4). I put on the whole armor of God (Ephesians 6:10-20), and I resolve to stand firm in my faith and resist the evil one.

6. I believe that apart from Christ I can do nothing (John 15:5), so I will depend totally on Him. I choose to remain in Christ in order to bear much fruit and glorify the Lord (John 15:8). I announce to Satan that Jesus is my Lord (1 Corinthians 12:3), and I reject any counterfeit gifts or works of Satan in my life.

7. I believe that the truth will set me free (John 8:32). I stand against Satan's lies by taking every thought captive in obedience to Christ (2 Corinthians 10:5). I believe that the Bible is the only reliable guide for my life (2 Timothy 3:15,16). I choose to speak the truth in love (Ephesians 4:15).

8. I choose to give my body to God to be used for righteousness, a living and holy sacrifice, and I choose to renew my mind by God's Word (Romans 6:13; 12:1,2). I put off the old self with its evil practices and put on the new self (Colossians 3:9,10). I am a new creature in Christ (2 Corinthians 5:17).

9. I ask my heavenly Father to fill me with His Holy Spirit (Ephesians 5:18), to lead me into all truth (John 16:13), and to give me power to live above sin and not carry out the desires of the flesh (Galatians 5:16). I crucify the flesh and choose to be led by and obey the Holy Spirit (Galatians 5:24).

10. I renounce all selfish goals and choose the ultimate goal of love (1 Timothy 1:5). I choose to obey the two greatest commandments: to love the Lord my God with all my heart, soul, and mind and to love others as myself (Matthew 22:37-39).

11. I believe that Jesus has all authority in heaven and on earth (Matthew 28:18) and that He rules over everything (Colossians 2:10). I believe that Satan and his demons are subject to me in Christ because I am a member of His body (Ephesians 1:19-23). I will obey God's command to submit to Him and to resist the devil (James 4:7). I command Satan in the name of Christ to leave my presence.

Step 3:
Bitterness Versus Forgiveness

If you do not forgive people who hurt you or offend you, you are a wide-open target for Satan's attacks. You need to forgive others so that Satan can't take advantage of you (2 Corinthians 2:10,11). We are to forgive others as God has shown us mercy and forgiven us (Luke 6:36; Ephesians 4:31,32).

Ask God to bring to your mind those you need to forgive as you read the following prayer aloud:

> Dear heavenly Father, thank You for Your kindness and patience which led me to turn from my sin (Romans 2:4). I have not always been kind, patient, and loving toward others, especially those who have hurt me. I have been bitter and resentful. I give You my emotions, and ask You to bring to the surface all my painful memories so I can choose to forgive from my heart. I ask You to bring to my mind the people I need to forgive (Matthew 18:35). I ask this in the precious name of Jesus, who will heal me from my hurts. Amen.

On a sheet of paper, make a list of the names which come to mind. Don't be surprised if your parents are near the top. In 95 percent of the people we lead through these steps, the first two names on the list are their parents.

The two most overlooked names on the lists are self and God. Forgiving yourself for your failures shows that you accept God's cleansing and forgiveness. Is it right to forgive God? He certainly hasn't done anything wrong—He can't. But maybe you cried out to Him with a need and He didn't seem to answer, so you are angry with Him. You may need to release Him for not living up to your false expectations.

Before you pray to forgive the people on your list, here are a few important things you need to understand about forgiveness:

Forgiveness is not forgetting. People who try to forget the pain caused by others often find they cannot. God says He will remember our sins no more (Hebrews 10:17). But God knows everything, and He can't forget. "Remember our sins no more" means that God will never use our sins against us (Psalm 103:12). You may not be able to forget your past, but you can be free from it. When we bring up the past and use it against others, we haven't forgiven them.

Forgiveness is a choice. We may feel that it's impossible to forgive someone. But since God requires us to forgive, it is something we can do. God would never require us to do something we cannot do. We forgive by choosing to forgive.

Forgiveness means giving up on revenge. Forgiveness is sometimes hard for us because we want revenge for the hurts we have suffered. But we are told never to take our own revenge (Romans 12:19). "Why should I let them off the hook?" we argue. When we forgive, we let them off *our* hook, but they aren't off *God's* hook. He will deal with them fairly, something we can't do.

If we don't let the offenders off our hook, we are hooked to them and our hurts. We can stop the pain by letting go of the problem. We don't forgive someone just for their sake; we do it for *our* sake so we can be free. Your need to forgive isn't an issue between you and the person who hurt you; it's between you and God.

Forgiveness is agreeing to live with the consequences of another person's sin. It costs us something to forgive. We pay the price for the hurt we forgive. We are going to live with the consequences whether we want to or not. Our only choice is whether we will do so in the bondage of bitterness or the freedom of forgiveness.

How do we forgive from our heart? First, we must admit the hurt and hatred we feel instead of burying them deep inside. If forgiveness doesn't include our emotions, it will be incomplete. You may not know how to deal with your feelings, but God does. Let Him bring the pain to the surface so He can deal with it. This is where the healing begins.

Since God has forgiven everyone on your list, you can too. This doesn't mean that you have to put up with continuing sin. It's possible to forgive the sins of the past and take a stand against the sins of the present.

Don't wait to forgive until you feel like forgiving. You will never get there. Feelings take time to heal, after the choice to forgive is made and Satan has lost his place (Ephesians 4:26,27).

For each person on your list pray aloud:

> Lord, I forgive (name) for (specifically name all his or her offenses and your painful memories that come to your mind).

Keep praying about each person until you are sure that all the pain you remember has been dealt with.

Positive feelings will follow in time; freeing yourself from the hurts of the past is the important issue.

Step 4:
Rebellion Versus Submission

We live in rebellious times. Many young people today don't respect or submit to the authorities God has placed over them. Christians are no exception. But rebelling against God, parents, and other authorities gives Satan an opportunity to attack.

The Bible tells us we have two responsibilities for the human authorities God has placed over us: pray for them and submit to them. The only time God permits us to disobey earthly leaders is when they order us to do something morally wrong before God. There are times when parents, other relatives, teachers, and others abuse their authority and break the laws which are ordained by God to protect innocent people. In such cases we need to seek help for our protection. When authorities abuse their position and ask us to break God's law or compromise our commitment to Him, we need to obey God, not man.

Study the following verses to understand how God wants us to respond to authority: civil government (Romans 13:1-7; 1 Timothy 2:1-4; 1 Peter 2:13-17); parents (Ephesians 6:1-3); employer (1 Peter 2:18-21); church leaders (Hebrews 13:17). Now pray the following prayer aloud:

> Dear heavenly Father, You have said in the Bible that rebellion is as bad as witchcraft, and disobedience is as sinful as serving false gods (1 Samuel 15:23). I know that I have disobeyed You by rebelling in my heart

against You and those You have put in authority over me. I ask Your forgiveness for my rebellion. By the shed blood of the Lord Jesus Christ I resist all evil spirits who took advantage of my rebellion. I pray that You will show me all the ways I have been rebellious. I choose to adopt a submissive spirit and servant's heart. In the name of Jesus Christ my Lord. Amen.

Being submissive to parents, teachers, and the government demonstrates faith. As we submit to God's line of authority, we are choosing to believe that God will protect us and bless us. Ask God to forgive you for those times you have not been submissive, and declare your trust in God to work through His line of authority by praying:

Lord, I agree I have been rebellious toward _____. Please forgive me for this rebellion. I choose to be submissive and obedient to Your Word. In Jesus' name. Amen.

Step 5:
Pride Versus Humility

Pride is a killer. Pride says, "I can do it! I can get myself out of this mess without God or anyone else's help." Oh no we can't! We absolutely need God, and we desperately need each other. Paul wrote: "We... worship in the Spirit of God and glory in Christ Jesus and put no confidence in the flesh" (Philippians 3:3). Humility is confidence properly placed. We are to "be strong in the Lord, and in the strength of His might"

(Ephesians 6:10). James 4:6-10 and 1 Peter 5:1-10 tell us that spiritual problems will follow when we are proud.

Use the following prayer to express your commitment to live humbly before God:

> Dear heavenly Father, You have said that pride goes before destruction and an arrogant spirit before stumbling (Proverbs 16:18). I confess that I have been thinking mainly of myself and not of others. I have not denied myself, picked up my cross daily, and followed You (Matthew 16:24). I have believed that I am the only one who cares about me, so I must take care of myself. I have turned away from You and have not let You love me. I am tired of living for myself and by myself. I now confess that I have sinned against You by placing my will before Yours and by centering my life around self instead of You. I renounce my pride and selfishness. I cancel any ground gained by the enemies of the Lord Jesus Christ. I ask You to fill me with Your Holy Spirit so I can do Your will. I give my heart to You and stand against all the ways that Satan attacks me. I ask You to show me how to live for others. I now choose to make others more important than myself and to make You the most important of all (Romans 12:10). I ask this in the name of Christ Jesus my Lord. Amen.

Having made that commitment, allow God to show you any specific areas in your life where you have been prideful. Check those which apply to you:

_____ I have a stronger desire to do my will than God's will.

_____ I rely on my own strength rather than God's.

_____ Too often I think my ideas are better than others'.

_____ I want to control others rather than develop self-control.

_____ Sometimes I consider myself more important than others.

_____ Sometimes I find it difficult to admit I was wrong.

_____ I am often a people-pleaser instead of a God-pleaser.

_____ I am overly concerned about getting the credit I deserve.

_____ I often think I am more humble than others.

_____ I often believe I am smarter than my parents.

_____ I often feel my needs are more important than the needs of others.

_____ Other:

For each statement that is true of you, pray the following prayer aloud:

Lord, I agree I have been prideful in the area of _____. Please forgive me for my pride. I choose to humble myself and place all my confidence in You. In Jesus' name. Amen.

Step 6:
Bondage Versus Freedom

The next step to freedom deals with sins which have become habits. Teens who have been caught in the trap of sin-confess-sin-confess may need to follow the suggestion of James 5:16: "Confess your sins to one another, and pray for one another, so that you may be healed. The effective prayer of a righteous man can accomplish much." Find a spiritually mature person who will hold you up in prayer and check up on you from time to time. Others may only need the assurance of 1 John 1:9: "If we confess our sins, He is faithful and righteous to forgive us our sins and to cleanse us from all unrighteousness."

Whether you need to confess to others or just to God, pray the following prayer:

> Dear heavenly Father, You have said, "Put on the Lord Jesus Christ, and make no provision for the flesh in regard to its lusts" (Romans 13:14). I understand that I have given in to fleshly lusts which wage war against my soul (1 Peter 2:11). I thank You that in Christ my sins are forgiven, but I have broken Your holy law and given the enemy an opportunity to wage war in my body (Romans 6:12,13; James 4:1; 1 Peter 5:8). I come before Your presence to admit these sins and to seek Your cleansing (1 John 1:9) that I may be freed from the bondage of sin. I now ask You to reveal to my mind the ways that I have broken Your moral law and disappointed the Holy Spirit. In Jesus' precious name I pray. Amen.

There are many sins of the flesh. You may want to open your Bible to Galatians 5:19-21 and pray through the verses, asking the Lord to reveal the ways you have specifically sinned.

It is our responsibility not to allow sin to control us by using our body as an instrument of unrighteousness (Romans 6:12,13). If you are struggling with habitual sexual sins (pornography, masturbation, sexual promiscuity, petting), pray as follows:

> Lord, I ask You to reveal to my mind every sexual use of my body as an instrument of unrighteousness. In Jesus' precious name I pray. Amen.

As the Lord brings to your mind every wrong sexual use of your body, whether it was done to you (for example, rape, incest, or any sexual molestation) or done willingly by you, renounce *every occasion.*

> Lord, I renounce (name the specific use of your body) with (name the person), and I renounce any bonding that may have taken place.

Now commit your body to the Lord by praying:

> Lord, I renounce all these uses of my body as an instrument of unrighteousness, and I confess any willful participation. I now present my body to You as a living sacrifice, holy and acceptable unto You, and I reserve the sexual use of my body for only the way You intended. I renounce the lie of Satan that my body is not clean, that it is

dirty or in any way unacceptable as a result of my past sexual experiences. Lord, I thank You that You have totally cleansed and forgiven me, that You love and accept me unconditionally. Therefore, I can accept myself. And I choose to do so, to accept myself and my body as cleansed. In Jesus' name. Amen.

Special Prayers for Specific Needs

Homosexuality

Lord, I renounce the lie that You have created me or anyone else to be homosexual, and I agree that You clearly forbid homosexual behavior. I accept myself as a child of God and declare that You created me a man (or woman). I renounce any bondages of Satan that have perverted my relationships with others. I announce that I am free to relate to the opposite sex in the way You intended. In Jesus' name. Amen.

Abortion

Lord, I confess that I was not a proper guardian and keeper of the life You entrusted to me, and I ask Your forgiveness. I choose to accept Your forgiveness by forgiving myself, and I now commit that child to You for Your care in eternity. In Jesus' name Amen.

Suicidal Tendencies

I renounce the lie that I can find peace and freedom by taking my own life. Satan is a thief, and he comes to steal, kill, and destroy. I choose life in Christ, who said He came to give me life and to give it abundantly.

Eating Disorders or Cutting on Yourself

I renounce the lie that my value as a person is dependent on how I look on the outside. I renounce cutting myself, vomiting, or using laxatives as a means of cleansing myself of evil, and I announce that only the blood of the Lord Jesus Christ can cleanse me from my sin. I accept the reality that there may be sin present in me because of the lies I have believed and the wrongful use of my body, but I renounce the lie that I am evil or that any part of my body is evil. I announce the truth that I am totally accepted by Christ, just as I am.

Substance Abuse

Lord, I confess that I have misused substances (alcohol, tobacco, food, prescription or street drugs) for the purpose of pleasure, to escape reality, or to cope with difficult problems. I confess that I have abused my body and programmed my mind in a harmful way. I have not allowed Your Holy Spirit to guide me. I ask Your forgiveness, and I renounce any satanic connection or influence in my life through my misuse of drugs. I cast my cares onto Christ who loves me, and I commit myself to no longer give in to substance abuse but to follow the Holy Spirit's leading. I ask You, heavenly Father, to fill me with Your Holy Spirit. In Jesus' name. Amen.

After you have confessed all known sin, pray:

I now confess these sins to You and claim, through the blood of the Lord Jesus Christ, my forgiveness and cleansing. I cancel all ground that evil spirits have gained through my willful involvement in sin. I ask this in the wonderful name of my Lord and Savior Jesus Christ. Amen.

Step 7:
Curses Versus Blessing

The last step to freedom is to turn your back on the sins of your ancestors (parents, grandparents, great-grandparents, etc.) and any curses which may have been placed on you. In giving the Ten Commandments, God said: "You shall not make yourselves any idols: any images resembling animals, birds, or fish. You must never bow to an image or worship it in any way; for I, the Lord your God, am very possessive. I will not share your affection with any other god! And when I punish people for their sins, the punishment continues upon the children, grandchildren, and great-grandchildren of those who hate me" (Exodus 20:4,5 TLB).

Evil spirits can be passed down to us from sinful members of the previous generations. We are not guilty of their sins, but because of these past sins Satan has gained a foothold in our families. We must renounce any sins and curses of our ancestors and claim our spiritual freedom in Christ.

In order to walk free from past influences, make the following declaration and pray the following prayer:

Declaration

I here and now reject and disown all the sins of my ancestors. As one who has been delivered from the kingdom of darkness into the kingdom of God's dear Son, I cancel out all demonic working that has been passed on to me from my ancestors. As one who has been crucified and raised with Jesus Christ and who sits with Him in heavenly places, I renounce all satanic assignments that are directed toward me, and I cancel every curse that Satan and his workers have put on me. I announce to Satan and all his forces that Christ became a curse for me (Galatians 3:13) when He died for my sins on the cross. I reject any and every way in which Satan may claim ownership of me. I belong to the Lord Jesus Christ who purchased me with His own blood. I reject all blood sacrifices whereby Satan may claim ownership of me. I declare myself to be eternally and completely signed over and committed to the Lord Jesus Christ. By the authority that I have in Jesus Christ, I now command every familiar spirit and every enemy of the Lord Jesus Christ that is in or around me to leave my presence. I commit myself to my heavenly Father, to do His will from this day forward.

Prayer

Dear heavenly Father, I come to You as Your child, purchased by the blood of the Lord Jesus Christ. You are the Lord of the universe and the Lord of my life. I submit my body to You as an instrument of righteousness, a living sacrifice, that I may glorify You in my body. I now ask You to fill me with Your Holy Spirit. I commit myself to the renewing of my mind in order to prove that Your will is good, perfect, and acceptable for me (Romans 12:2). All this I do in the name and authority of the Lord Jesus Christ. Amen.

Once you have secured your freedom by going through these seven steps, you may find demonic influences attempting reentry days or even months later. One person shared that she heard a spirit say to her mind, "I'm back" two days after she had been set free. "No, you're not!" she proclaimed aloud. The attack stopped immediately.

One victory doesn't mean that the war has been won. Freedom must be maintained. You will stay free as long as you remain in right relationship with God. If you should slip and fall, immediately get up and get right with God again.

One victim of incredible abuse shared this illustration: "Spiritual bondage is like being forced to play a game with an ugly stranger in my own home. I kept losing and I wanted to quit, but the ugly stranger wouldn't let me. Finally I called the police (a higher authority), and they came and escorted the stranger out. He knocked on the door trying to regain entry, but this time I recognized his voice and didn't let him in."

What a beautiful illustration of gaining freedom in Christ. We call upon Jesus, the highest authority in heaven and earth, and He escorts the enemy out of our lives. But it's our responsibility not to let him back in. We must know the truth, stand firm, and resist the evil one. Get involved in a church youth group and commit yourself to regular times of Bible study and prayer. God loves you, and He will never leave or forsake you.

Truth Encounter

Read: Galatians 5:1

Reflect: 1. Finding freedom in Christ is a result of confessing, forgiving, renouncing, and forsaking. Which of these areas is the most challenging for you?

2. Is there anything you can think of that would keep you from living free in Christ today? Are there any steps you feel you need to review?

3. What steps were the most meaningful or encouraging to you? Why?

4. In what ways do you think you could share this message of freedom with others who might be struggling?

Respond: Pray and thank God for the freedom He offers us. Also pray a prayer of commitment, that you will continue to grow and walk in freedom.

13

Living Free and Staying Free

The freedom you gained by walking through the steps to freedom in Chapter 12 must be maintained. You have won a very important battle; but the war goes on. Freedom is yours as long as you keep choosing truth and standing firm in the strength of the Lord. If old, unconfessed sins should surface, confess them. If you become aware of Satan's lies you have believed or remember other non-Christian experiences you have had, renounce them and choose the truth. Some people have found it helpful to work through the steps to freedom again. As you do, follow the instructions carefully.

In this chapter we'll look at six important Bible-based guidelines to help you maintain your freedom and walk with Christ. Be aware that we don't get any extra points with God if we follow these tips, nor do we lose points with Him if we ignore them. God loves us whether we follow His guidelines or not. However, His strong desire is that we choose to follow His guidelines and walk in freedom. Our reward for following these tips is the victory and freedom we will experience in our daily lives.

1. Strengthen Your Freedom with Fellowship

God never intended that we live the Christian life alone. That's why He created the church. Get involved with a good youth group where you can walk in the light and speak the truth in love with other growing Christians. Make sure it's a church where God's Word is taught clearly and accurately.

Hebrews 10:23-25 tells us: "Let us hold fast the confession of our hope without wavering, for He who promised is faithful; and let us consider how to stimulate one another to love and good deeds, not forsaking our own assembling together, as is the habit of some, but encouraging one another; and all the more, as you see the day drawing near."

Verse 25 warns us not to "forsake our own assembling together." We are to build each other up in our faith, and that happens when we worship, pray, and study God's Word together. If we avoid going to church and meeting with other Christians, we become weak and vulnerable to the enemy's attack.

Hebrew 3:13 instructs us to "encourage one another day after day," not just on Sundays or whenever the youth group meets. We need to treat other Christians as our brothers and sisters in Christ and help one another in areas we need to grow.

2. Strengthen Your Freedom by Studying God's Word

The primary way to get to know God is to get to

know His Word, the Bible. Reading good Christian books and listening to Christian music is great, but they are no substitute for reading and studying God's Word. There are many easy-to-read youth Bibles around for you to use. Your freedom in Christ will really be encouraged as you get into God's Word, study it, and memorize key verses.

In the Old Testament, Ezra was a man greatly used by God. In fact, we're told that "the hand of the LORD his God was upon him" (Ezra 7:6). Ezra made God's Word a big part of his life. Verse 10 says, "Ezra had set his heart to study the law of the LORD, and to practice it." Do you want God's hand on you? Set your heart to study God's Word and practice it.

It's a good idea to set a certain time each day to study your Bible and pray. If you're a "rooster" (an early-riser), the morning may be a good time for you because you're fresh and alert. If you're a "night owl" (a late-nighter), you may do better reading before you go to bed. Select a quiet, comfortable place where you won't be interrupted or distracted—but not so comfortable that you struggle to stay awake!

This special time Christians set aside to study God's Word and pray is often called a "quiet time." Use your daily quiet time to read, study, and reflect on what God's Word has to say to you. The apostle Paul writes, "All Scripture is inspired by God and profitable for teaching, for reproof, for correction, for training in righteousness; that the man of God may be adequate, equipped for every good work" (2 Timothy 3:16,17). Therefore "be diligent to present yourself approved to God as a workman who does not need to be ashamed, handling accurately the word of truth" (2 Timothy 2:15).

3. Strengthen Your Freedom Through Daily Prayer

Proverbs 15:8 tell us, "The Lord . . . delights in the prayers of his people" (TLB). Because of the relationship we have with God through Christ's death, burial, and resurrection, we are free to talk to God anytime we like. And we can talk to Him about anything— friends, homework, parents, problems. Commit yourself to talk to God every day, not just during your quiet time but anytime.

Here are some sample prayers you can pray often and with confidence.

A Prayer for Daily Life

Dear heavenly Father, I honor You as my Lord. I know that You are always present with me. You are the only all-powerful, all-knowing God. You are kind and loving in all Your ways. I love You and thank You that I am united with Christ and spiritually alive in Him. I choose not to love the world, and I put to death all my sinful desires. I thank You for the life that I now have in Christ, and I ask You to fill me and guide me with Your Holy Spirit so I can live my life free from sin. I declare my dependence upon You, and I take my stand against Satan and all his lying ways. I choose to believe the truth, and I refuse to be discouraged. You are the God of all hope, and I am confident that You will meet my needs as I seek to live according to Your Word. I am confident that I can live a responsible life through Christ who strengthens me. I now take my stand against Satan and command him and all his evil spirits to depart from me. I put on the armor of God. I submit my body as a living sacrifice and renew my mind by the living Word of God in order that I may prove that the will of God is good, acceptable, and perfect. I ask these things in the precious name of my Lord and Savior Jesus Christ. Amen.

Bedtime Prayer

Thank You, Lord, that You have brought me into Your family and have blessed me with every spiritual blessing in the heavenly realm in Christ. Thank You for providing this time of rest through sleep. I accept it as part of Your perfect plan for me, and I trust You to guard my mind and my body during my sleep. As I have thought on You and Your truth during this day, I choose to let those thoughts continue in my mind while I am asleep. I commit myself to You for Your protection from every attempt of Satan or his demons to attack me during sleep. I commit myself to You as my rock, my fortress, and my resting place. I pray in the strong name of the Lord Jesus Christ. Amen.

A Prayer for a Home or Room

Pray this prayer aloud after removing all articles of false worship from your room or home.

Heavenly Father, I know that You are Lord of heaven and earth. In Your power and love, You have given me all things to enjoy. Thank You for this place to live. I claim this home/room for my family/me as a place of spiritual safety and protection from all the attacks of the enemy. As a child of God in Christ, I command all evil spirits claiming territory because of the activities of previous occupants to leave and never return. I renounce all curses and spells against this place. I ask You, heavenly Father, to post guardian angels around this home/room to guard it from the attempts of the enemy to enter and disturb Your purposes for us/me. I thank You, Lord, for doing this, and pray in the name of the Lord Jesus Christ. Amen.

4. Strengthen Your Freedom by Taking Every Thought Captive

If we want to stay free in Christ, we must assume responsibility for our own thought life. Second Corinthians 10:5 instructs us to take every thought captive to the obedience of Christ. In order to remain free, we must reject the lies, choose the truth, and stand firm in our position in Christ.

Remember, we are not trying to dispel the darkness; we are trying to turn on the light. The way you overcome a lie is by choosing the truth. The way to overcome anxious thoughts is to turn to God and then do what Paul says:

Finally, brethren, whatever is true, whatever is honorable, whatever is right, whatever is pure, whatever is lovely, whatever is of good repute, if there is any excellence and if anything worthy of praise, let your mind dwell on these things. The things you have learned and received and heard and seen in me, practice these things; and the God of peace shall be with you (Philippians 4:8,9).

If you come under direct attack, say out loud to Satan and his demons, "I command you to leave my presence in the name of the Lord Jesus Christ." Don't *ask* him to leave; *tell* him to leave in the authority of Christ: "Satan, in the name of Jesus Christ, get out of here right now." If you are paralyzed by fear and can't seem to say anything, then inwardly call upon the Lord. He knows the "thoughts and intentions of the heart" (Hebrews 4:12). Submit to God first, then resist the devil (James 4:7).

Also, keep your mind from drifting away. It's very easy to get lazy in your thinking and revert back to old thought patterns. Share your struggles openly with a trusted friend or a youth leader. Paul writes, "Brethren, do not be children in your thinking; yet in evil be babes, but in your thinking be mature" (1 Corinthians 14:20).

5. Strengthen Your Freedom by Understanding Who You Are in Christ

We will grow in freedom as we continue to understand and accept our identity and worth in Christ.

How can we do that? By filling our mind with the truth from God's Word about our acceptance, security, and significance in Christ.

The following statements summarize our scriptural identity and position in Christ and form the foundation for our freedom in Christ. Read these statements aloud often. Whenever you are involved in a spiritual conflict, read these statements aloud at least once each day for a month.

Who Am I?

I am the salt of the earth (Matthew 5:13).

I am the light of the world (Matthew 5:14).

I am a child of God (John 1:12).

I am part of the true vine, and Christ's life flows through me (John 15:1,5).

I am Christ's friend (John 15:15).

I am chosen by Christ to bear fruit (John 15:16).

I am Christ's personal witness sent out to tell everybody about Him (Acts 1:8).

I am a slave of righteousness (Romans 6:18).

I am a slave to God, making me holy and giving me eternal life (Romans 6:22).

I am a child of God; I can call Him my Father (Romans 8:14,15; Galatians 3:26; 4:6).

I am a coheir with Christ, inheriting His glory (Romans 8:17).

I am a temple—a dwelling place—for God. His Spirit

and His life live in me (1 Corinthians 3:16; 6:19).

I am joined forever to the Lord and am one spirit with Him (1 Corinthians 6:17).

I am a part of Christ's body (1 Corinthians 12:27).

I am a new person. My past is forgiven and everything is new (2 Corinthians 5:17).

I am at peace with God, and He has given me the work of helping others find peace with Him (2 Corinthians 5:18,19).

I am a child of God and one with others in His family (Galatians 3:26,28).

I am a child of God and will receive the inheritance He has promised (Galatians 4:6,7).

I am a saint, a holy person (Ephesians 1:1; Philippians 1:1; Colossians 1:2).

I am God's handiwork, created in Christ to do His work (Ephesians 2:10).

I am a citizen of heaven with all of God's family (Ephesians 2:19).

I am a prisoner of Christ to help others (Ephesians 3:1; 4:1).

I am righteous and holy (Ephesians 4:24).

I am a citizen of heaven seated in heaven right now (Philippians 3:20; Ephesians 2:6).

I am hidden with Christ in God (Colossians 3:3).

I am an expression of the life of Christ because He is my life (Colossians 3:4).

I am chosen of God, holy and dearly loved (Colossians 3:12; 1 Thessalonians 1:4).

I am a child of light and not of darkness (1 Thessalonians 5:5).

I am chosen to share in God's heavenly calling (Hebrews 3:1).

I am part of Christ; I share in His life (Hebrews 3:14).

I am one of God's living stones, being built up in Christ as a spiritual house (1 Peter 2:5).

I am a member of a chosen race, a royal priesthood, a holy nation, a people belonging to God (1 Peter 2:9,10).

I am only a visitor to this world in which I temporarily live (1 Peter 2:11).

I am an enemy of the devil (1 Peter 5:8).

I am a child of God, and I will be like Christ when He returns (1 John 3:1,2).

I am born again in Christ, and the evil one—the devil —cannot touch me (1 John 5:18).

I am *not* the great "I am" (Exodus 3:14; John 8:24, 28,58), but by the grace of God, I am what I am (1 Corinthians 15:10).

Since I am in Christ, by the grace of God...

I am now acceptable to God (justified) and completely forgiven. I live at peace with Him (Romans 5:1).

The sinful person I used to be died with Christ, and sin no longer rules my life (Romans 6:1-6).

I am free from the punishment (condemnation) my sin deserves (Romans 8:1).

I have been placed into Christ by God's doing (1 Corinthians 1:30).

I have received God's Spirit into my life. I can recognize the blessings He has given me (1 Corinthians 2:12).

I have been given the mind of Christ. He gives me His wisdom to make right choices (1 Corinthians 2:16).

I have been bought with a price; I am not my own; I belong to God (1 Corinthians 6:19,20).

I am God's possession, chosen and secure in Him (sealed). I have been given the Holy Spirit as a promise of my inheritance to come (2 Corinthians 1:21,22; Ephesians 1:13,14).

Since I have died, I no longer live for myself, but for Christ (2 Corinthians 5:14,15).

I have been made acceptable to God (righteous) (2 Corinthians 5:21).

I have been crucified with Christ and it is no longer I who live, but Christ lives in me. The life I now live is Christ's life (Galatians 2:20).

I have been blessed with every spiritual blessing (Ephesians 1:3).

I was chosen in Christ to be holy before the world was created. I am without blame before Him (Ephesians 1:4).

I was chosen by God (predestined) to be adopted as His child (Ephesians 1:5).

I have been bought out of slavery to sin (redeemed) and forgiven. I have received His generous grace (Ephesians 1:6,7).

I have been made spiritually alive just as Christ is alive (Ephesians 2:5).

I have been raised up and seated with Christ in heaven (Ephesians 2:6).

I have direct access to God through the Spirit (Ephesians 2:18).

I may approach God with boldness, freedom, and confidence (Ephesians 3:12).

I have been rescued from the dark power of Satan's rule and have been brought into the kingdom of Christ (Colossians 1:13).

I have been forgiven of all my sins and set free. The debt against me has been canceled (Colossians 1:14).

Christ Himself lives in me (Colossians 1:27).

I am firmly rooted in Christ and am now being built up in Him (Colossians 2:7).

I am fully grown (complete) in Christ (Colossians 2:10).

I have been buried, raised and made alive with Christ (Colossians 2:12,13).

I died with Christ and I have been raised up with Christ. My life is now hidden with Christ in God. Christ is now my life (Colossians 3:1-4).

I have been given a spirit of power, love, and self-control (2 Timothy 1:7).

I have been saved and set apart (sanctified) according to God's plan (2 Timothy 1:9; Titus 3:5).

Because I am set apart (sanctified) and one with Christ, He is not ashamed to call me His brother or sister (Hebrews 2:11).

I have the right to come boldly before the throne of God. He will meet my needs lovingly and kindly (Hebrews 4:16).

I have been given great and valuable promises. God's nature has become a part of me (2 Peter 1:4).*

6. Strengthen Your Freedom Through Sharing Your Faith

Young people in your church and on your campus really need the Lord and the freedom He has to offer. You have the privilege and responsibility of telling others how you came to know Christ as Savior and how you came to experience your freedom in Christ. First Peter 3:15 says, "Quietly trust yourself to Christ your Lord and if anybody asks why you believe as you do, be ready to tell him, and do it in a gentle and respectful way" (TLB).

The strongest witness for Christ is to walk in His ways and live in His freedom. Colossians 2:6,7 tell us, "As you therefore have received Christ Jesus the Lord, so walk in Him, having been firmly rooted and now being built up in Him and established in your faith."

You are qualified to witness and share your freedom because of who you are in Christ. You have

---

* Neil Anderson and Dave Park, *Stomping Out the Darkness* (Ventura, CA: Regal Books, 1993). Used by permission.

God's Spirit and God's Word. Together you and the Holy Spirit make a great team. Peter said in Acts 5:32, "We are witnesses of these things; and so is the Holy Spirit, whom God has given to those who obey Him." Successful witnessing is simply going to other people in the power of the Holy Spirit and confidently sharing with them the truths of the Bible through the story of how you came to know Christ and found your freedom in Him.

Pray for your non-Christian friends and those who have trusted Christ but are not walking in the freedom the Lord has to offer. Ask God to open doors of opportunity for you to share your faith and freedom. Remember: It's your responsibility to share, but it's the Holy Spirit's responsibility to move people's hearts to accept Christ or to make the choice to walk in His freedom. You can't fail unless you let Satan deceive you into not sharing your story.

Don't let Satan silence you through the fear of rejection or embarrassment. If you are experiencing these fears, be aware that they are not from God, because "God has not given us a spirit of timidity [fear], but of power and love and discipline" (2 Timothy 1:7). The apostle Peter puts it this way:

> And who is there to harm you if you prove zealous for what is good? But even if you should suffer for the sake of righteousness, you are blessed. And do not fear their intimidation, and do not be troubled, but sanctify Christ as Lord in your hearts, always being ready to make a defense to everyone who asks you to give an account for the hope that is in you, yet with gentleness and

reverence; and keep a good conscience (1 Peter 3:13-16).

It is our hope that through this book you have met Jesus Christ the Bondage Breaker and that through Him you have been set free. Other than eternal life, freedom in Christ is your most precious possession. It's freedom from your past. You're free to be yourself and free to grow in Christ. Jesus suffered the shame of the cross so you could be alive and free in Him. He will always be there for you so that you can live and stay free in Christ.

Truth Encounter

Read: 2 Timothy 3:15-17; Philippians 4:8,9; Hebrews 10:23-25

Reflect: 1. Why does our freedom need to be maintained? What should you do if you remember an old, unconfessed sin?

2. How does fellowship with other Christians help our walk of freedom? Why is studying God's Word so important to our freedom?

3. How is our thought life related to staying free? Why is understanding who you are in Christ so vital?

4. How did you feel after you read the "Who Am I?" list? Will anything on that list ever change?

Respond: Pray and ask for God's guidance to use the authority He has given you to win the battle for the mind and to walk in freedom. Make a commitment to read the "Who Am I?" list daily and use the follow-up prayers.

For more information about Freedom in Christ Youth Ministries or the resources they have to offer, please write or call:

Freedom in Christ Youth Ministries
491 E. Lambert Road
La Habra, CA 90631
Phone: (310) 691-9128

More books from Neil Anderson to help you and those you love find freedom in Christ.

- ***Victory Over the Darkness***
  Regal Books

- ***The Bondage Breaker***
  Harvest House Publishers

- ***The Bondage Breaker Study Guide***
  Harvest House Publishers

- ***Spiritual Warfare*** (Timothy M. Warner)
  Crossway Books

- ***Winning Spiritual Warfare***
  Harvest House Publishers

- ***Walking in the Light***
  Thomas Nelson Publishers

- ***The Seduction of Our Children***
  Harvest House Publishers

- ***Released from Bondage***
  Thomas Nelson Publishers

- ***Breaking Through to Spiritual Maturity***
  Regal Books

- ***Living Free in Christ***
  Regal Books

- ***Stomping Out the Darkness***
  Regal Books

- ***The Bondage Breaker, Youth Edition***
  Harvest House Publishers

- ***Daily in Christ***
  Harvest House Publishers

To find out more, please write or call us at
FREEDOM IN CHRIST MINISTRIES
491 E. Lambert Road, La Habra, California 90631
Phone (310) 691-9128 • FAX (310) 691-4035

Freedom in Christ Ministries

Purpose: *Freedom in Christ Ministries is an interdenomiational, international, Bible-teaching Church ministry which exists to glorify God by equipping churches and mission groups, enabling them to fulfill their mission of establishing people free in Christ.*

Freedom in Christ Ministries offers a number of valuable video, audio, and print resources that will help both those in need and those who counsel. Among the topics covered are:

Resolving Personal Conflicts

Search for Identity ■ *Walking by Faith* ■ *Faith Renewal* ■ *Renewing the Mind* ■ *Battle for the Mind* ■ *Emotions* ■ *Relationships* ■ *Forgiveness*

Resolving Spiritual Conflicts

Position of Believer ■ *Authority* ■ *Protection* ■ *Vulnerability* ■ *Temptation* ■ *Accusation* ■ *Deception & Discernment* ■ *Steps to Freedom*

Spiritual Conflicts and Biblical Counseling

Biblical Integration ■ *Theological Basis* ■ *Walking by the Spirit* ■ *Surviving the Crisis* ■ *The Process of Growth* ■ *Counseling and Christ* ■ *Counseling the Spiritually Afflicted* ■ *Ritual Abuse*

The Seduction of Our Children

God's Answer ■ *Identity and Self-Worth* ■ *Styles of Communication* ■ *Discipline* ■ *Spiritual Conflicts and Prayer* ■ *Steps to Freedom*

Resolving Spiritual Conflicts and Cross-Cultural Ministry
Dr. Timothy Warner

Worldview Problems ■ *Warfare Relationships* ■ *Christians and Demons* ■ *The Missionary Under Attack* ■ *Practical Application for Missionaries* ■ *Steps to Freedom in Christ*

Other Good
Harvest House Reading

THE BONDAGE BREAKER
by *Neil Anderson*

Jesus intends for us to win the spiritual battles that confront us daily and He has provided everything we need to gain the victory. Yet instead of experiencing victory, we often find ourselves trapped in defeat—overcome with frustration, bitterness, and discouragement. If you have ever found yourself enslaved by negative thought patterns, controlled by irrational feelings, or caught in habitual sinful behavior, Neil Anderson can help you understand the strategy of Satan and fight back.

CLASSIC CHRISTIANITY
Life's Too Short to Miss the Real Thing!
by *Bob George*

In his down-to-earth style, Bob George shares the road back to joy and contentment in the Christian life. Clearly outlining the common pitfalls and misconceptions that hinder and rob so many Christians today, Bob confronts the question of why so many Christians start out as enthusiastic believers and then decide that Christianity doesn't "work" for them. He then provides the truth that will help Christians get back on track and stay there.

RADICAL RESPECT
by *Jim Burns*

In a society permeated by sex and permissiveness, straight answers to questions about sexuality are still hard to come by. In *Radical Respect*, noted youth pastor Jim Burns balances straightforward discussion of real-life situations with God's original plan for sexuality.

Dear Reader:

We would appreciate hearing from you regarding this Harvest House nonfiction book. It will enable us to continue to give you the best in Christian publishing.

1. What most influenced you to purchase *The Bondage Breaker, Youth Edition*?
   - ☐ Author
   - ☐ Subject matter
   - ☐ Backcover copy
   - ☐ Recommendations
   - ☐ Cover/Title
   - ☐ _____

2. Where did you purchase this book?
   - ☐ Christian bookstore
   - ☐ General bookstore
   - ☐ Department store
   - ☐ Grocery store
   - ☐ Other

3. Your overall rating of this book:
   - ☐ Excellent   ☐ Very good   ☐ Good   ☐ Fair   ☐ Poor

4. How likely would you be to purchase other books by this author?
   - ☐ Very likely
   - ☐ Somewhat likely
   - ☐ Not very likely
   - ☐ Not at all

5. What types of books most interest you?
   (check all that apply)
   - ☐ Women's Books
   - ☐ Marriage Books
   - ☐ Current Issues
   - ☐ Self Help/Psychology
   - ☐ Bible Studies
   - ☐ Fiction
   - ☐ Biographies
   - ☐ Children's Books
   - ☐ Youth Books
   - ☐ Other _____

6. Please check the box next to your age group.
   - ☐ Under 18
   - ☐ 18-24
   - ☐ 25-34
   - ☐ 35-44
   - ☐ 45-54
   - ☐ 55 and over

Mail to: Editorial Director
Harvest House Publishers
1075 Arrowsmith
Eugene, OR 97402

Name _____

Address _____

City _____ State _____ Zip _____

**Thank you for helping us to help you
in future publications!**